DR GEMMA PYBUS
UNLOCKING SEARCH INTENT
YOUR KEY TO ONLINE RELEVANCE

BALBOA.PRESS
A DIVISION OF HAY HOUSE

Copyright © 2024 Dr Gemma Pybus.

All rights reserved. No part of this book may be used or reproduced by any means, graphic, electronic, or mechanical, including photocopying, recording, taping or by any information storage retrieval system without the written permission of the author except in the case of brief quotations embodied in critical articles and reviews.

Balboa Press books may be ordered through booksellers or by contacting:

Balboa Press
A Division of Hay House
1663 Liberty Drive
Bloomington, IN 47403
www.balboapress.co.uk
UK TFN: 0800 0148647 (Toll Free inside the UK)
UK Local: (02) 0369 56325 (+44 20 3695 6325 from outside the UK)

Because of the dynamic nature of the Internet, any web addresses or links contained in this book may have changed since publication and may no longer be valid. The views expressed in this work are solely those of the author and do not necessarily reflect the views of the publisher, and the publisher hereby disclaims any responsibility for them.

The author of this book does not dispense medical advice or prescribe the use of any technique as a form of treatment for physical, emotional, or medical problems without the advice of a physician, either directly or indirectly. The intent of the author is only to offer information of a general nature to help you in your quest for emotional and spiritual well-being. In the event you use any of the information in this book for yourself, which is your constitutional right, the author and the publisher assume no responsibility for your actions.

Any people depicted in stock imagery provided by Getty Images are models, and such images are being used for illustrative purposes only.
Certain stock imagery © Getty Images.

Print information available on the last page.

ISBN: 978-1-9822-8859-4 (sc)
ISBN: 978-1-9822-8858-7 (e)

Library of Congress Control Number: 2024907099

Balboa Press rev. date: 05/03/2024

Contents

Acknowledgements vii
Introduction ix

Chapter 1	The Evolution of Intent 1
Chapter 2	Unveiling the Power of Search Intent in the AI Era 15
Chapter 3	Uncovering Some of the Factors Influencing Search Results 25
Chapter 4	Understanding User Intent 35
Chapter 5	The Psychology of Intent 53
Chapter 6	Intent-Based Keyword Research 71
Chapter 7	Intent-Driven Content Marketing 97
Chapter 8	Intent and SEO 107
Chapter 9	Intent-Based Paid Advertising 121
Chapter 10	Ethical Considerations in Intent-Based Marketing 131
Chapter 11	The Practical Application of Intent-Based Keyword Research 147
Chapter 12	Digital Marketing Glossary 151

About the Author 155

Acknowledgements

Special thanks to my wonderful husband, James Pybus, our fantastic children (James, Lily, and Molly), and the rest of my family for their support as I complete something far more useful and sensible than getting my chainsaw licence, swimming with sharks, or dressing up as a dinosaur.

Thanks too to the University of West London's Claude Littner Business School, in particular, my long-suffering students and most excellent and inspirational colleagues Mike O'Brien, Max Stricker, and Jonathan Gabay, from whom I have learnt so much.

Thanks also to the fantastic Digital Groundworks team—James (again!), Neville Gibbons, Scott Saunders-Singer, John Russell, Peter Hoffman, and Kosta Tashkov.

Introduction

The power of the Web is in its universality. Access by everyone regardless of disability is an essential aspect.
—Tim Berners-Lee, inventor of the World Wide Web

Tim Berners-Lee envisioned a digital landscape of equality and universal access, but four decades later, the reality is one of complexity and personalisation. The Web as we know it is a kaleidoscope, shifting and changing to match the eyes of the beholder. In the following pages, we consider the mysterious world of search engines, those silent puppeteers of information, and their impact on human intent (and vice versa). Search engines can tailor a world of information unique to each user with their 'secret sauce' algorithms blending location, device, search history, and more to deliver the perfect search results to every searcher. Because of this, we'll consider the following question: When we search the Web, are we uncovering the universe of knowledge or merely a mirror reflecting our biases and boundaries? We also discuss the concept of intent, another factor the search engines are increasingly using to present us with the most appropriate online information.

Have you ever stopped to question the intent behind our actions online? The motivations that drive us, the desires that push us forward, and the conscious and unconscious decisions we make daily as we navigate the Web for business and leisure. Intent is the invisible force that guides our thoughts, shapes our behaviours, and ultimately determines our destinies. From the courtroom to the digital marketplace, intent plays a pivotal role in shaping our decisions, influencing our search for products, and ultimately driving our purchasing choices.

For some, the concept of intent is deeply entwined with criminal law. We have grown accustomed to associating intent with criminal acts, with the notion of mens rea—the guilty mind. But what happens when we step outside the confines of the courtroom and into the vast expanse of the online world? How does intent manifest when searching for products, comparing options, and deciding whether and what to purchase?

It is crucial to recognise that our understanding of intent is dynamic. Just as the concept has evolved within the framework of criminal law, so too has it evolved in the context of consumer behaviour. In the following pages, we explore how intent can be influenced by social influence, advertising, and even the algorithms that shape our online experiences. We delve into the psychology behind our decision-making processes, uncovering the underlying motivations that drive us to click, browse, and purchase.

In this age of information overload, navigating the world of consumer intent has become a complex task. We are bombarded with advertisements, targeted marketing messages, and a seemingly endless array of choices. How do we make sense of it all? How do we ensure that our intentions align with our values and desires?

This book is not just a theoretical exploration of intent and an investigation into the impact of search engines on human behaviour. It is a practical guide for marketers, content creators, business owners, and anyone involved in keyword research, search engine optimisation, and paid search advertising. It provides valuable insights into leveraging intent to create engaging content, drive organic and paid-for traffic, and ultimately increase conversion rates.

So, join me on this expedition into the realm of search engines and human intent. Together, we will navigate the complex web of consumer behaviour, uncovering the hidden forces that drive us to search, click, and ultimately purchase.

Chapter 1
THE EVOLUTION OF INTENT

Intent in Criminal Law

Though the topic of intent in criminal law may seem a strange place to start in a book predominantly about finding success in the search engine results pages, I need you to trust me! Intent is an abstract, conceptual notion that can be difficult to grasp and verbalise, so starting with clear and concise definitions—like those outlined in criminal law—is excellent for exploring this multifaceted topic.

Intent is a fundamental concept in criminal law, a key element in determining guilt or innocence and establishing a defendant's state of mind. It is the mental element or mindset that accompanies an act that is prohibited by law. In simple terms, intent refers to the purpose or intention behind committing a crime.

In criminal law, intent is defined as a conscious desire or purpose to commit a specific criminal act. It involves a mental state whereby the person knows the consequences of their actions and intends to bring about those consequences. Mens rea is the term used to describe this intent and is described by *The Oxford English Dictionary* as 'The particular

1

state of mind required to make an action criminal; a criminal state of mind; (more generally) criminal intent' (Oxford University Press, 2023).

The legal system distinguishes between different levels of intent, such as specific intent and general intent. Specific intent refers to situations whereby the defendant intends to cause a particular result. In contrast, general intent relates to situations whereby the defendant intends to commit an act without regard to a specific outcome.

There are various categories of intent recognised in criminal law. Direct intent refers to situations in which the defendant specifically intends to cause a particular result. Indirect intent, conversely, refers to situations in which the defendant does not explicitly intend the result but foresees that it is a likely consequence of their actions. Transferred intent occurs when the defendant intends to harm one person but harms another.

Proving intent in criminal cases can be challenging since it involves establishing the defendant's state of mind. The burden of proof lies with the prosecution, who must present evidence to convince the court of the defendant's intention to commit the crime. Direct evidence, such as the defendant's confession, may be available in some cases. However, intent is often inferred from circumstantial evidence, such as the defendant's actions, statements, and prior behaviour.

To understand intent further, it is essential to differentiate between intent and motive in criminal law.

While motive refers to the underlying reason or justification for committing a crime, intent focuses on the defendant's mental state at the time of the act. Intent is considered a more crucial factor in determining culpability as it directly relates to the defendant's mindset and conscientious decision to commit the crime.

An example of intent determining guilt can be seen in the case of the chief constable of Avon and Somerset versus Shimmen (1987),[1] a martial arts expert who was demonstrating his advanced high-kick skills to companions but miscalculated the move and broke a shop window. The defendant said he only meant to bring his foot close to the window, mere inches from the glass. However, he was found guilty of causing criminal damage as the argument that he was not reckless (due to giving thought to the potential outcome of his actions and believing the risk to be minimal) was rejected since it was argued that he knew there was some risk involved in his action yet proceeded to do it.

As you can see, motive and intent are intertwined and difficult to understand, let alone prove conclusively. Proving intent can be incredibly challenging due to the intrinsic nature of mental states. The defendant's intention cannot be directly observed, making it necessary to rely on circumstantial evidence. Courts often address these

---

[1] 'Chief Constable of Avon and Somerset versus Shimmen: Case Summary' (2022) IPSA LOQUITUR. Available at https://ipsaloquitur.com/criminal-law/cases/chief-constable-avon-somerset-v-shimmen/ (accessed 1 January 2024).

challenges by considering the totality of the evidence and drawing reasonable inferences from the defendant's conduct and surrounding circumstances. However, there is still widespread debate on the issue. As a result, it is difficult for all involved in passing judgements and sentencing (including the jury) to have a consistent understanding of what constitutes criminal intent.

Our understanding of intent continues to evolve, reflecting societal changes and advancements in science and psychology. By exploring its applications beyond criminal law, we gain a deeper appreciation of intent's role in our lives and understand that intent cannot be directly and objectively observed. In digital marketing, as in criminal law, we need to consider all the data available to us from social media platforms, resources like Google Analytics and Search Console, primary marketing research, and so on to make decisions that are as objective and informed as possible about the intentions of our existing and potential customers.

Intent in Online Search

In today's digital age, online search has become an integral part of our daily lives. Search engines like Google, Bing, and Yahoo connect users with the information they seek. Whether finding a recipe, researching a topic, or buying a product, online search has revolutionised how we access information. However, understanding user intent is paramount for search engines to deliver relevant results effectively. Without a clear understanding of what users are looking for, search engines would be ineffective in providing valuable information.

In the context of online search, intent refers to a user's underlying motivation or goal. It goes beyond the keywords used and delves into the deeper meaning behind the search query. For instance, a user searching for 'best restaurants in Aylesbury' may want to find a good place to eat out, while another user searching for 'how to cook spaghetti' may have the goal of learning a new recipe. Understanding user intent is crucial for search engines to provide relevant and accurate results.

Search engine algorithms have come a long way in interpreting user intent. In the early days of search engines, results were primarily based on keyword matching, often leading to irrelevant or spammy content appearing at the top of search results. However, machine learning and artificial intelligence (AI) advancements have enabled search engines to better understand user intent. Algorithms now consider user behaviour, location, and search history to deliver more personalised and relevant results.

Search engines employ various methods and techniques to determine user intent. One of these methods is query analysis, which involves analysing the search query to understand the user's intent. This analysis considers the words used, the order in which they are presented, and any additional context provided. User behaviour analysis is another technique used to infer user intent. By analysing factors such as click-through rates, engagement rates, and time spent on a page, search engines can gain insights into what users find most relevant and valuable. Additionally, contextual signals such as location, device type, and language preferences, help search engines understand user intent.

User intent has a profound impact on how search engine algorithms prioritise search results. Search engines aim to deliver the most relevant results to users as this increases user satisfaction and retention. By interpreting and accurately understanding user intent, search engines can rank pages higher in search results. This also incentivises marketers to optimise their content to align with user intent and improve their search visibility.

Search engines go to great lengths to tailor search results based on user intent. They analyse various factors to personalise search results, including user location, device type, and search history. By considering these factors, search engines can provide users with more relevant content that aligns with their intents. For example, users searching for 'coffee shops near me' will receive results specific to their current locations.

Semantic search is a branch of search that focuses on understanding the meaning behind search queries rather than simply matching keywords. Intent plays a crucial role in semantic search as it helps search engines provide more accurate results. By using natural language processing (NLP) and entity recognition, search engines can better understand user intent and deliver more relevant search results. For example, a search for 'Who won the FIFA Men's World Cup in 2022?' involves understanding the user's intent to find the most recent winner of the Men's Football World Cup competition.

As technology continues to evolve, so does the understanding of user intent in online search. Advancements in machine learning, NLP, and voice recognition are likely to further enhance the ability of search engines to interpret and anticipate user intent. Search results will become even more personalised and tailored to individual users. Marketers must stay informed about these developments and adapt their strategies to remain competitive in the ever-changing digital landscape.

Intent in Consumer Behaviour

Understanding consumer intent and decision-making processes allows marketers to effectively target and engage with their audiences, leading to better sales and customer satisfaction outcomes. This makes it an incredibly valuable concept to understand in digital marketing.

Consumer intent can be defined as the underlying motivation or purpose behind a consumer's decision to engage in a particular behaviour, such as making a purchase. It encompasses the thoughts, emotions, and considerations influencing the consumer's decision-making process.

Different forms of consumer intent can be identified, each with its influence on purchasing behaviour.

Informational intent refers to the consumer's goal of seeking information or knowledge about a product or service. Navigational intent involves the consumer's intention to find a website or webpage. Transactional intent is characterised by the consumer's desire to complete a specific transaction, such as purchasing. Lastly, social intent pertains to the consumer's intention to connect with others or seek social validation through purchasing decisions.

To effectively target and engage consumers, marketers must first identify their intents. Various methods and tools can be used to gain insights into consumer intent. Data analysis, market research, and customer surveys are valuable tools that provide marketers with important information about consumer intent. Understanding consumer demographics, preferences, and motivations is crucial.

Once consumer intent is identified, marketers can tailor their strategies to align with the specific intent of their target audience. Marketers can effectively engage with consumers and increase conversions by utilising targeted messaging, personalised recommendations, and customised offers.

Understanding consumer intent is closely linked to customer journey mapping. By mapping the customer journey (from needs awareness, where a customer first discovers the need for a product or service, through to conversion, where the customer decides to purchase an item), marketers can identify the key touchpoints where consumer intent plays a crucial role. Aligning marketing efforts with consumer intent at each journey stage enhances engagement, conversion, and customer loyalty. By recognising the different stages consumers go through when making purchase decisions, marketers can effectively guide them towards their desired outcome.

When it comes to content marketing, understanding consumer intent is incredibly important. By comprehending the specific intent of the target audience, marketers can create and distribute relevant and valuable content that addresses the consumer's needs and desires. Conducting keyword research, trend analysis, and social listening can help identify consumer intent and inform content creation strategies. The ability to provide the right content at the right time significantly increases the chances of capturing the consumer's attention and influencing the decision-making process.

Consumer intent also plays a vital role in search engine optimisation (SEO) strategies. Search engines strive to deliver users the most relevant search results based on their intent. Marketers can improve search engine rankings and visibility by optimising website content, metadata, and structure to align with consumer intent. Techniques such as utilising long-tail keywords and semantic search allow marketers to target specific consumer intent and enhance their online presence effectively.

Understanding consumer intent is vital in improving the user experience on websites and digital platforms. By incorporating intuitive navigation, relevant content, and personalised recommendations, marketers can better meet consumer intent and enhance overall satisfaction. User testing and analytics provide valuable insights into consumer intent and guide user experience optimisation.

Consumer intent can be leveraged to optimise conversion rates. Marketers can significantly increase conversions by employing persuasive design, clear calls to action, and optimised landing pages that align with consumer intent. A/B testing and data analysis are pivotal in identifying and refining strategies based on consumer intent, ensuring optimal results.

As you can see, intent is a critical concept to investigate and apply to your digital marketing activities. It ties into every single digital channel out there, from websites to social media. We will discuss best practice recommendations for some of these channels later in the book. Before we do, it's important to consider how we can measure the increased success of our marketing activities once we have considered customer intent more comprehensively. The answer lies in conversion rates.

Intent and Conversion Rates

Conversion rates refer to the percentage of website visitors or users who complete a desired action, such as purchasing, signing up for a newsletter, or filling out a form. They are a crucial metric for determining the success of marketing campaigns. The higher the conversion rate, the more successful the campaign is considered to be. Marketers need to set clear conversion goals and track conversions to evaluate their strategies' effectiveness and, therefore, understand the impact that careful consideration of consumer intent has on their digital marketing activities.

User intent plays a significant role in influencing conversion rates. Different types of intent—such as informational, navigational, and transactional intent—can significantly impact the likelihood of conversions. For example, users with informational intent may seek information to carefully consider and be less likely to convert immediately, while users with transactional intent may be ready to purchase immediately. By understanding and targeting the specific intent of their audience, marketers can effectively tailor their messaging and offers to increase the chances of conversion.

The Future of Intent

Our understanding of intent in digital marketing, as in criminal law, is constantly developing. As AI continues to advance, it will undoubtedly play a pivotal role in shaping how we understand and harness user intent. AI-powered algorithms and machine-learning techniques have proven their efficacy in analysing user behaviour, preferences, and interactions to predict intent more accurately. By delving deep into vast datasets, AI can unlock invaluable insights into the desires and motivations that drive users, enabling marketers to create personalised and relevant experiences that resonate on a profound level.

One notable trend reshaping the future of intent is the rise of voice search. With the advent of voice-activated virtual assistants like Siri and Alexa, the way we search for information is changing. Voice search introduces a new dimension to user intent as the spoken word often reveals more nuanced, conversational queries. This necessitates a shift in marketing strategies, requiring marketers to optimise for voice queries and understand the subtleties of intent in this unique context. By adapting to these changes, marketers can ensure that their content is discoverable and tailored to the ever-changing landscape of user intent.

Data analytics will continue to be a fundamental component in understanding and predicting user intent in the future. Advanced analytics tools and techniques can provide valuable insights into user behaviour and preferences and allow us to develop ideas about consumer intent. By analysing data at scale and employing predictive analytics, marketers can stay one step ahead in understanding the evolving landscape of user intent and deliver personalised experiences that truly resonate with their audience.

Amidst the exciting technological advancements, it is crucial to remember that the human factor remains vital in the future of intent. Empathy, creativity, and emotional intelligence are essential to connecting with users. Despite the advancements in AI and machine learning, understanding the intricacies of the human psyche and motivations remains crucial in effective intent-driven marketing. By combining technological advances with human insights, marketers can unlock the true power of intent and forge meaningful connections with their audiences.

In conclusion, the future of intent is a captivating and ever-evolving landscape. As digital marketers, it is essential to stay informed and adaptable, embracing emerging technologies and trends to harness the power of user intent in our marketing efforts. By understanding and personalising experiences based on user intent, we can increase conversions, enhance customer satisfaction, and foster long-term relationships with our audiences. The future holds incredible possibilities, and by applying the strategies and techniques discussed in this book, marketers can unlock the full potential of user intent and achieve remarkable results in their campaigns.

Chapter 2
UNVEILING THE POWER OF SEARCH INTENT IN THE AI ERA

Before we begin to investigate search intent online, we need to start with the basics and understand the tools we use daily to search for information and products online—search engines.

What Are Search Engines?

Search engines serve as the virtual librarians of the internet, tirelessly sifting through the endless sea of data to deliver relevant and valuable results to users. Comprehending the keywords and terms associated with search engines is crucial for navigating this digital landscape with confidence and efficacy.

Before we embark on this journey, let us first acquaint ourselves with a set of fundamental terms that will form the foundation of our understanding of search engines:

1. Web crawlers
2. Indexes
3. Algorithms

Web crawlers, also known as spiders or bots, are the unsung heroes behind the scenes of search engines. These digital creatures tirelessly traverse the Web, systematically visiting webpages and indexing their content. Their primary function is to gather data, which is then used by search engines to provide accurate and up-to-date search results to users.

Indexes, in the context of search engines, refer to the vast repositories of information gathered and organised by Web crawlers. These indexes serve as the backbone of search engines, allowing for quick and efficient retrieval of relevant information in response to user queries.

Algorithms are the secret sauce that powers search engines. These complex mathematical formulas analyse the indexed data and determine the most relevant and authoritative results for a given search query. They consider many factors, including keyword relevance, website credibility, user location, and search history to deliver personalised and tailored results to each user. In 2009, one Google developer advised that there were two hundred variables considered by their search engine when determining a page's position in the search engine results pages. Consider how many are likely to be considered now, fifteen years later.

Imagine the Web as a colossal library, with web crawlers acting as diligent librarians, meticulously cataloguing the content of each book. The indexes are like a library's meticulously organised card catalogue, allowing for swift retrieval of relevant information. The algorithms function as the insightful and wise reference librarian who, armed with knowledge of individual preferences and interests, guides each visitor to the most pertinent and compelling books.

As we immerse ourselves in the intricate world of search engines, it becomes evident that these technological marvels are not merely tools for information retrieval but dynamic gateways to personalised knowledge and understanding.

The Evolution of Search Engines

To truly appreciate the present state of search engines, we need to consider how far they have come since the dawn of the internet. Early in the history of the World Wide Web, search engines were rudimentary but laid the foundation for what was to come. The likes of Archie, Gopher, and early versions of Yahoo! and AltaVista pioneered organising and indexing the vast amounts of information available on the internet. These early search engines primarily relied on manual categorisation and essential keyword matching to provide users with relevant results. While they may seem archaic by today's standards, their contributions cannot be underestimated as they set the stage for the sophisticated algorithms that would follow.

The introduction of algorithmic search marked a turning point in the evolution of search engines. With the emergence of Google's PageRank algorithm, search engines adopted a more analytical approach to understanding user intent. PageRank revolutionised SEO by leveraging link analysis, effectively ranking the relevance of webpages based on their interconnectedness. This breakthrough allowed search engines to provide users with more accurate and trustworthy results. The development of ranking algorithms became crucial in deciphering user intent as they aimed to match search queries with the most relevant information available.

However, despite the advancements made in algorithmic search, challenges in understanding user intent persisted. One of the significant hurdles search engines faced was keyword ambiguity. User search queries often lacked specificity, leading to result pages that catered to multiple interpretations of intent. Additionally, relevancy issues arose as search engines strove to differentiate between information merely related to the query and information that genuinely addressed the user's intent. To overcome these challenges, search engines needed to develop more sophisticated algorithms to interpret user queries contextually and provide precise results.

Over time, search engine algorithms evolved and became increasingly sophisticated in interpreting user intent. Simple keyword matching gave way to semantic search, enabling search engines to understand the meaning behind user queries. As machine learning advanced, algorithms became more adept at incorporating user behaviour, search history, and location data into their decision-making processes.

These advancements significantly improved search engines' ability to comprehend and anticipate user intent, leading to more relevant and personalised search results.

With the rise of personalised search results, search engines began tailoring their recommendations to individual users. By analysing user preferences, location, and previous search history, search engines could provide highly personalised search experiences. This personalisation enhanced search results' relevance and reflected a greater understanding of user intent. It allowed search engines to anticipate user needs and provide recommendations aligned with their interests, making the search experience more intuitive and tailored.

Today, AI has become an integral component of search engines. AI-powered algorithms contribute to a deeper understanding of user intent by analysing vast amounts of data and identifying patterns. Natural language-understanding algorithms can now contextualise search queries, capturing subtle nuances and delivering results that address the user's intent. Powered by AI, contextual search considers a user's search history, location, and preferences, further refining the understanding of search intent. As AI continues to advance, search engines have the potential to improve their ability to anticipate and fulfil user intent with unmatched precision.

What Is AI?

The world of algorithms and artificial intelligence can be a challenge to understand even if you are technologically savvy. So before we go any further into establishing how AI can help us unlock the secrets of user intent, let's take a step back and consider the topic of AI to develop an understanding of how it is possible for a machine to make meaningful judgements about human intent.

The quest to create intelligent machines can be traced back to ancient civilisations, where mythological tales and folklore depicted artificial beings endowed with humanlike qualities. However, it was not until the emergence of modern computing technologies that the concept of AI began to materialise into a tangible pursuit.

The earliest origins of AI can be found in the musings of visionaries such as Ada Lovelace and Alan Turing, who laid the theoretical foundations for machine intelligence in the nineteenth and twentieth centuries. Lovelace's visionary insights into the potential for machines to perform beyond mere calculation and Turing's seminal work on computability and the concept of the Turing test set the stage for the formal exploration of AI.

The mid-twentieth century witnessed significant milestones in the development of AI with the creation of the first artificial neural network by Frank Rosenblatt in the 1950s and the birth of the field of NLP with the development of the ELIZA program in the mid-1960s.

These breakthroughs laid the groundwork for subsequent advancements in AI, leading to the development of expert systems, robotics, and machine learning in the latter half of the twentieth century.

The turn of the twenty-first century heralded a new era of AI innovation marked by the emergence of deep learning techniques, the proliferation of big data, and the integration of AI into everyday technologies. The creation of IBM's Watson, the triumph of AlphaGo in defeating human champions in the game of Go, and the rapid advancements in NLP exemplify the transformative impact of AI on various domains.

Today, AI has permeated virtually every facet of human existence, from personalised recommendation systems to autonomous vehicles and medical diagnostics. The convergence of AI with search engine technologies has created new possibilities for content generation and dissemination, reshaping the digital information ecosystem and redefining the parameters of human–machine interaction.

However, the rise of AI has been accompanied by challenges and controversies. Ethical dilemmas surrounding the use of AI in decision-making, concerns over algorithmic bias and data privacy, and the existential implications of AI on human autonomy and free will have sparked intense debate surrounding the responsible deployment of intelligent systems. Nevertheless, AI is becoming a key consideration when determining consumer intent in digital marketing.

The Role of AI in Search Intent

AI technologies, such as NLP and machine learning, have revolutionised how we understand and cater to user intent in search queries. The sheer volume and complexity of online content make it increasingly challenging for search engines to determine user intent and deliver precise results accurately. However, AI has emerged as a game-changer, enabling more accurate and efficient search-intent analysis.

NLP forms the backbone of AI-powered search-intent analysis. Using sophisticated algorithms, NLP enables machines to process and interpret human language, extracting meaning and intent from search queries. This involves understanding the context, recognising language nuances, and deciphering the true intention behind the words. By incorporating NLP into search engines, AI technologies can analyse the semantic structure of search queries, discern user preferences, and deliver more relevant search results.

Machine learning, another cornerstone of AI, plays a vital role in search-intent analysis. By training machine-learning algorithms on vast amounts of data, search engines can identify patterns and trends in user search queries. This enables a better understanding of user intent, leading to more accurate search results. Machine-learning algorithms can adapt and evolve, continuously improving their knowledge of user intent based on user behaviour and feedback.

However, it is essential to acknowledge the limitations of AI in search-intent analysis. Language nuances, colloquialisms, and context understanding can challenge AI algorithms. There is also the potential for biased results as AI algorithms learn from existing data that may carry inherent biases. Therefore, ongoing improvements and human oversight are crucial for addressing these limitations and ensuring the ethical use of AI in search-intent analysis.

The advancements in deep learning, natural language understanding, and neural networks have unlocked immense potential for AI technologies in search-intent analysis. These technologies contribute to a better understanding and prediction of user intent, bridging the gap between what users want and what search engines deliver. With deep learning, search engines can uncover hidden patterns and associations, allowing for more precise search results. Natural language understanding enables search engines to comprehend user queries contextually, leading to more accurate interpretations. Neural networks, on the other hand, empower search engines to model complex relationships and reproduce the intricacies of human thought processes. Together, these AI technologies promise a future of search-intent analysis that is insightful, personalised, and highly relevant to individual users.

Chapter 3

UNCOVERING SOME OF THE FACTORS INFLUENCING SEARCH RESULTS

As we delve deeper into understanding search engine algorithms and how they present information to users based on their complex calculations regarding user intent, it becomes increasingly evident that many factors influence the search results generated by a user query. These factors encompass diverse elements such as location, device, browser, and search history. These elements are pivotal in shaping the personalised search experience for users, and their significance lies in their ability to tailor search algorithms to achieve results according to individual preferences and contextual relevance.

Location plays a crucial role in influencing search results by customising them based on the geographical proximity of the user to the subject matter. This localisation enhances the relevance of search results, especially for queries related to local businesses, services, or events. Similarly, device type—whether desktop, mobile, or tablet—dictates the presentation and prioritisation of search results to ensure optimal user experience across different devices.

Browser preferences further contribute to personalised

search results by considering the user's browsing history, cookies, and saved preferences to tailor the search experience. Additionally, search history, encompassing past queries and interactions, significantly influences search results by adapting to the user's search habits and preferences.

While location customises search results based on geographical relevance, device type and browser preferences influence the formatting and presentation of search results. The contrast lies in the role each factor plays in tailoring the results' content or optimising their display to suit the user's device and browsing preferences. Search history, on the other hand, personalises results based on the individual's past interactions, creating a unique search experience for each user.

The analysis of these factors reveals the intricate web of personalisation and customisation woven into the fabric of search engine algorithms. By integrating location, device, browser, and search history, search engines strive to deliver tailored results that align with the user's context, preferences, and past interactions. This customisation enhances the relevancy of search results and enriches the user experience by presenting content in a format and context that resonates with individual needs.

The Importance of Location in Search Engine Results Page (SERP) Listings

To deliver the most relevant content to users, search engines are increasingly prioritising localised results to deliver more relevant and personalised information to users. Understanding how search engine algorithms determine which pages make it to the SERPs for users in different areas is pivotal for marketers and businesses aiming to optimise online visibility.

At the heart of this localisation emphasis lies the profound shift in user behaviour. As mobile devices become ubiquitous, users frequently search on the go, seeking information pertinent to their immediate surroundings. This shift has prompted search engines to incorporate location-based signals into their algorithms, tailoring results based on where users are geographically situated.

Google, for instance, utilises a multifaceted approach to determine the relevance of a page to users in specific locations. One key factor is the user's IP address, which provides a broad indication of their geographic location. Additionally, Google Business Profiles can play a crucial role in the search results presented to users. Local businesses with accurate and up-to-date Google Business profiles are more likely to appear prominently in local search results. This is particularly pertinent for companies with physical storefronts or service areas as local SEO efforts can significantly influence their visibility in SERPs.

Search engines also analyse the content of webpages to discern their relevance to local searches. Location-specific keywords, references to local landmarks, and other geographically relevant content contribute to a page's likelihood of appearing in the SERPs for users in the corresponding area. For example, a bakery in Aylesbury optimising its content for 'best buns in Buckinghamshire' is more likely to be featured prominently when users in that county search for such delicacies.

The significance of location in SERP listings is further underscored by the rise of 'near me' searches. Users increasingly rely on search engines to find immediate solutions in their vicinities, whether it's a restaurant, a gym, or a service provider. Search engines respond by prioritising businesses that align with the user's proximity, emphasising the critical role of location-based optimisation.

For marketers and businesses, recognising and capitalising on this emphasis on location is strategic. Local SEO becomes an essential tool in the arsenal for enhancing online visibility. This involves optimising content with location-specific keywords, cultivating positive local reviews, engaging with local communities on social media, and ensuring accurate and consistent business information across online platforms.

In conclusion, the importance of location in SERP listings is a testament to the evolving nature of search engine algorithms and user behaviour. As search engines increasingly prioritise localised results, businesses and marketers must strategically optimise their online presence to align with these preferences. Understanding the intricate mechanisms by which search engines determine SERP rankings for users in different areas is not just a competitive advantage; it's an essential element of a successful digital marketing strategy in the contemporary landscape.

Device-Specific Search Factors

The importance of device type in shaping SERP listings has emerged as another issue worthy of discussion when contemplating the impact on user experience. As users access search engines through an array of devices, ranging from traditional desktops to mobile phones and tablets, search algorithms are becoming increasingly sophisticated in tailoring results to suit the characteristics of each device. Understanding how search engine algorithms operate based on device type is essential for businesses and marketers seeking to optimise their online presence and engage users effectively. One of the fundamental dynamics in this landscape is the shift towards mobile-centric experiences. With the pervasive use of smartphones, search engines, notably Google, have transitioned to a mobile-first indexing approach. This means that the mobile version of a website is prioritised over its desktop counterpart when determining SERP rankings. For businesses, this underscores the critical importance of mobile optimisation.

Mobile-friendly websites not only cater to the preferences of an increasing number of users but also align with search engine algorithms that prioritise mobile responsiveness. Factors like page loading speed, mobile-friendly design, and seamless navigation on smaller screens contribute to a positive user experience, positively impacting SERP rankings for mobile searches.

Beyond mobile optimisation, the diversity of devices in use further complicates the SERP landscape. For example, tablet users may have distinct preferences and behaviours compared to those on smartphones or desktops. Search algorithms may consider different screen sizes, capabilities, and usage patterns to deliver tailored results for each device.

As the internet of things (IoT) continues to expand, with devices ranging from smart speakers to wearable gadgets becoming common, the intricacies of device-centric search experiences will likely become more nuanced. Marketers must stay attuned to emerging technologies and user behaviours to adapt their strategies accordingly.

In conclusion, the importance of device type in SERP listings reflects the diverse ways users access information in the digital age. Mobile optimisation is no longer an option but a necessity, and businesses must align their strategies with the preferences and behaviours associated with various devices. Recognising the impact of device type on search engine algorithms empowers marketers to craft strategies that resonate with users across different platforms, enhancing their visibility and relevance in an increasingly mobile-centric online landscape.

The Importance of Browsing History on Search Engine Results

As we've previously discussed, search engines favour delivering personalised results to users based on many factors, and a user's browsing history plays a central role in this personalisation. When a user is signed into a Google account, their search history, including past queries, clicked links, and visited websites, is tracked and analysed. Search algorithms then use this wealth of data to tailor future search results to align with the user's preferences and historical engagement patterns.

One fundamental way browsing history influences SERP listings is by prioritising websites with which the user has previously engaged. If a user frequently visits a particular website or clicks on specific types of content, search algorithms interpret this behaviour as a signal of relevance and preference. Consequently, the algorithm is likelier to display pages from these familiar sources higher in the SERPs, aiming to provide a personalised and satisfying search experience.

Conversely, a user's lack of engagement with certain websites or content types is also considered by search algorithms. If a user consistently avoids clicking on links from a particular domain or ignores specific topics, the algorithm interprets this behaviour as an indication of disinterest. As a result, the SERP listings for that user may be adjusted to minimise the visibility of content they have historically shown little interest in.

The impact of browsing history on SERP listings extends beyond the individual user. Aggregated data from a broader user base enables search engines to identify trending topics, popular websites, and emerging trends. This collective intelligence informs algorithmic adjustments at a macro level, influencing the ranking and visibility of websites for users who share similar interests or search patterns.

However, the utilisation of browsing history in SERP listings has sparked discussions about user privacy and data protection. While personalised search results enhance user experience, they raise concerns about how user data is collected and used. In response, search engines have implemented privacy features, allowing users to control or delete their search histories and manage personalised settings.

Adapting to the nuances of personalised search results is crucial for marketers and businesses. Content strategies should consider the importance of engaging users consistently to build positive signals in their browsing histories. This involves creating high-quality relevant content that resonates with the target audience and encourages continued engagement.

In conclusion, the importance of a user's browsing history in SERP listings highlights the evolution of search algorithms towards personalisation. As search engines strive to deliver tailored and relevant results, the user's past behaviour guides their future search experiences. For businesses and marketers, navigating this landscape involves a delicate balance between understanding user preferences, delivering valuable content, and respecting privacy concerns in the ever-evolving digital terrain.

Chapter 4
UNDERSTANDING USER INTENT

As discussed earlier, there are many categories of consumer intent. When we are browsing online, we may simply be looking for information, comparing products and services, or actively purchasing to name but a few types of online user intent. We need to understand the differences between these intentions to ensure we present website users with relevant information and encourage them to buy from us either immediately or by introducing a consumer to our brand and ethos and conveying the benefits of our products and services so they are more likely to buy from us in the future. In this chapter, we discuss the different types of user intent in more detail.

Navigational Intent

The first category of intent we consider is navigational intent. Understanding navigational intent is a crucial aspect of successful online marketing strategies. Navigational intent refers to the mindset of users actively seeking a specific website or brand. Understanding navigational intent is like holding the key to unlocking the potential of your target audience. By optimising your online presence to capture these users, you can dramatically increase brand visibility and customer engagement and ultimately drive conversions.

Branding plays a fundamental role in influencing navigational intent. A strong brand presence can stimulate curiosity and evoke trust in potential customers, leading them to seek a particular website intentionally. Brands that have effectively cultivated a recognised and trusted image can significantly influence users to search for their website directly rather than rely on generic search terms. One famous technology company, for example, has mastered navigational intent with their iconic logo and consistent branding across all traditional and digital touchpoints. Even without explicitly saying it, seeing an apple with a bite taken from it is synonymous with accessing its website and products.

To optimise online presence for navigational intent, marketers must implement strategies that enhance the user experience and make it easier for users to find their desired websites. Firstly, having a user-friendly website with straightforward navigation and intuitive design is paramount. A clutter-free interface with well-organised menus and easily accessible information will help users swiftly locate the websites they are searching for. Additionally, implementing proper SEO techniques—including on-page and off-page activities like incorporating relevant keywords in the metadata on the page and improving page load speed—can significantly enhance a website's visibility in search engine results. By carefully crafting these aspects, marketers can maximise the chances of capturing users with navigational intent.

In the realm of navigational intent, delivering a seamless and memorable user experience is paramount. Users with clear intent when searching for a particular website are likely to navigate through a site offering a positive user experience. This includes user interface design, website speed, and mobile optimisation. A visually appealing and intuitive interface will captivate users and ensure easy navigation and swift access to desired information. Furthermore, website speed is critical to creating a positive user experience. Slow-loading pages can quickly deter users, leading them to abandon their searches and turn to competitors. Lastly, optimising websites for mobile devices is no longer an option but a necessity in today's mobile-first world. Websites must be fully responsive and adapt to different screen sizes to provide an exceptional user experience across all devices. By focusing on these elements, marketers can cultivate a memorable user experience that keeps users engaged and encourages them to return.

Social media platforms have become powerful tools for marketers looking to optimise their online presence for navigational intent. By actively maintaining engaging social media profiles, brands can maximise their reach and direct users to their desired websites. Consistently posting relevant, shareable content fosters brand recognition and encourages users to seek the website directly. With their strong social media presence and interactive content, brands like Nike have effectively leveraged social media platforms to capture users with navigational intent. By creating a robust online community and continually providing value to their followers, Nike has fostered a sense of loyalty that drives users to actively search for their website.

Tracking and analysing user behaviour is crucial for optimising online presence. By gathering data on user behaviour, marketers can gain valuable insights into how users interact with websites and identify patterns that can inform decision-making. Tools such as Google Analytics and heat-mapping software provide detailed information on user engagement, time spent on each page, and conversion rates. These insights help marketers understand the effectiveness of their strategies and make informed decisions to continuously improve their online presence for navigational intent.

Optimising online presence for navigational intent is a critical competency for marketers. By understanding the concept of navigational intent, leveraging branding, implementing effective strategies, creating a memorable user experience, leveraging social media platforms, and analysing user behaviour, marketers can unlock the potential of their target audience. The ability to capture users with intent, guiding them directly to the desired website or brand, is the hallmark of a successful digital marketing campaign. As we continue our exploration of intent, let us delve further into the realms of informational and transactional intent, expanding our understanding of the intricate interplay between human psychology and purchase decisions.

Informational Intent

The next category of intent we consider is informational intent. In a world where users constantly seek answers and solutions to their queries, providing valuable content to meet their informational needs becomes the key to connecting and engaging with them. Informational intent refers to users looking for information, whether to learn something new, solve a problem, or gain insights.

User informational intent can take various forms, ranging from specific how-to queries to more research-based inquiries. The motivations behind this intent can also be diverse, with users seeking knowledge and understanding or wanting to address a problem or make an informed decision. Marketers must delve into the multifaceted nature of informational intent, understanding the underlying motivations and providing content that caters to these needs. Marketers can effectively align their strategies and content to meet user expectations by identifying and understanding the different types of informational intent.

Creating content that meets informational intent requires careful consideration of several vital elements. First and foremost, providing accurate, reliable, and up-to-date information is essential. Users rely on the content they find trustworthy and credible. As marketers, it is our responsibility to deliver on these expectations. Secondly, the content should be concise, well-structured, and easily understood. Complex ideas can be broken into digestible pieces using language that resonates with the intended audience. By focusing on these elements, marketers ensure that their content effectively meets the informational intent of users.

In meeting users' informational intent, research-based content plays a significant role. Marketers can establish themselves as credible sources in their respective industries by conducting in-depth research and providing comprehensive and authoritative information. This can be achieved by incorporating statistics, case studies, and expert opinions, all of which enhance the credibility and reliability of the content. By going beyond surface-level information, marketers can meet the informational intent of users who seek a deeper understanding of a particular subject.

How-to guides and tutorials are beneficial when meeting users' informational intent. These forms of content provide step-by-step instructions and clear visuals that guide users through a process or help them accomplish a task. By anticipating and addressing potential questions and concerns, marketers can ensure that their how-to guides and tutorials effectively meet the informational needs of users. This not only empowers users but also positions brands as helpful and reliable sources of information.

To cater to the diverse needs of users with informational intent, marketers must leverage different content formats.

Blog posts, articles, videos, and infographics, among others, can all be utilised to deliver valuable information that resonates with the target audience. Choosing the suitable format depends on factors such as the nature of the information and the preferences of the audience. Incorporating multimedia elements like images and videos can enhance user engagement, making the content more captivating and easily digestible.

Optimising content to meet informational intent involves various strategies to ensure visibility and relevance. By utilising relevant keywords that reflect users' informational queries, marketers can increase the chances of their content appearing in search engine results. Optimising meta-tags, headings, and URLs also improves the visibility of the content, making it more likely to be clicked by users. Effective optimisation ensures the content reaches its intended audience, connecting users with valuable information and fulfilling their informational intent.

As with any marketing effort, measuring success in informational intent marketing is crucial. Metrics and key performance indicators (KPIs) provide valuable insights into marketing strategies and content effectiveness. Monitoring user engagement metrics, such as time on page and engagement rates, can help gauge the level of interest and relevance of the content. Tracking conversions and leads generated from informational intent marketing campaigns measures the impact and effectiveness of the strategies employed.

Informational intent holds immense power in shaping purchase decisions and influencing consumer behaviour. As digital marketers, it is our responsibility to understand and cater to the informational needs of users. We can successfully meet users' informational intent by creating valuable, accurate, and reliable content, optimising it for visibility, and measuring its effectiveness.

Transactional Intent

The next category of intent we consider is transactional intent. Transactional intent is a critical concept in the realm of digital marketing. Recognising and leveraging this specific type of intent is crucial for marketers to effectively engage with their target audiences and lead them towards making a purchase. In this subchapter, we explore the intricacies of transactional intent and delve into the strategies that can be employed to capitalise on this powerful motivator.

Transactional intent, as its name implies, refers to the mindset and behaviour of users actively seeking to make a purchase. These individuals are driven by strong motivation and a sense of urgency to find a product or service that fulfils their needs or desires. They have moved beyond the initial awareness and research stages and are now ready to act. Understanding the nature and characteristics of users with transactional intent is crucial for marketers to effectively engage and convert them into customers.

To effectively engage with users with transactional intent, it is essential to understand their journeys towards purchasing. This journey typically begins with their initial awareness of a product or service followed by research, evaluation, and comparison. As marketers, we must identify the key touchpoints along this journey and provide relevant and persuasive information at each stage to guide users towards the desired outcome. By understanding their journeys, we can effectively meet their needs and desires and influence their purchase decisions.

Creating compelling offers is one of the most effective ways to engage and convert users with transactional intent. These offers can take various forms, such as discounts, promotions, limited-time deals, or added value. By understanding the specific needs and desires of users with transactional intent, we can tailor our offers to address their pain points and provide them with a compelling reason to make a purchase.

Calls to action (CTAs) are crucial in driving conversions from users with transactional intent. These CTAs must be crafted to resonate with the users' desires and motivations. For example, using clear and concise language, creating a sense of urgency, and emphasising the benefits of taking action can all contribute to the effectiveness of a CTA. By understanding the psychology of users with transactional intent, we can create CTAs that compel them to take the desired action and ultimately make a purchase.

Landing pages serve as the gateway to conversion for

users with transactional intent. It is essential to optimise these pages to maximise conversions and minimise bounce rates. By following best practices in design, layout, copywriting, and the placement of calls to action, we can create landing pages that engage users and guide them towards purchasing. A compelling headline, an intuitive and user-friendly layout, persuasive copy, and a prominent call to action are all essential elements to consider when optimising landing pages for conversion.

Social proof is a powerful motivator for users with transactional intent. We can build trust and credibility with our target audiences by showcasing positive customer reviews, testimonials, case studies, or endorsements. Users are more likely to purchase when they see that others have had positive experiences and can validate their decision. By effectively leveraging social proof, we can tap into its influence on transactional intent and increase conversions.

Building trust and credibility is crucial when targeting users with transactional intent. We can establish ourselves as trusted authorities in our respective industries by showcasing industry awards, certifications, and accreditations and highlighting relevant customer success stories. Transparent pricing and policies further enhance the perception of trustworthiness and can significantly impact a user's decision-making process. Building trust is a continuous effort that requires consistently delivering quality products and services and effective communication with our target audiences.

The checkout process is a crucial stage for users with transactional intent, and optimising this process is paramount to reducing friction and increasing conversions. By streamlining the checkout experience, offering multiple payment options, and providing clear progress indicators, we can enhance the user experience and minimise the chances of cart abandonment. A user-friendly and seamless checkout process can significantly impact conversion rates and contribute to the overall success of our marketing efforts.

Users with transactional intent may not always purchase on their first visit to a website. Retargeting and remarketing strategies can be crucial in converting these users who may have initially abandoned their purchases. By staying top of mind with potential customers through targeted ads and personalised messaging, we can re-engage them and increase the likelihood of conversion. Retargeting and remarketing are potent techniques for leveraging the transactional intent of users and nudging them towards making a purchase.

Once again, measuring conversion success is vital for understanding the impact of our marketing strategies on users with transactional intent. Key metrics and analytics tools can provide valuable insights into conversion rates, ROI, and other performance indicators. By continuously monitoring and analysing these metrics, we better understand what is working and what needs improvement.

In conclusion, transactional intent is a powerful motivator significantly influencing purchase decisions. By creating compelling offers, crafting persuasive CTAs, optimising landing pages, leveraging social proof, building trust, optimising the checkout process, and employing retargeting and remarketing strategies, we can tap into the transactional intent of users and increase conversions. Measuring conversion success, studying case studies, and success stories further strengthen our understanding of transactional intent and guide future marketing endeavours.

Commercial Investigation Intent

In this subchapter, we delve into the behaviour of users who compare products or services before making a decision. This is a crucial stage in the consumer journey, and marketers need to understand this intent to distinguish their offerings from competitors effectively. We refer to this type of intent as 'Commercial Investigation Intent'.

To comprehend commercial investigation intent, we must first define and understand its nuances. It involves users driven by a desire to compare various products or services. These individuals seek to gather information and evaluate alternatives to make an informed decision. Their motivations can vary, ranging from securing the best deal to ensuring their product choice is the best quality available. Factors such as cost, quality, features, and reputation play significant roles in influencing this intent.

When engaging in commercial investigation intent, users go through a decision-making process. It begins with problem recognition, where they identify a need or desire for a particular product or service. This leads to an information search, where they seek relevant information through various channels such as search engines, social media, and consumer reviews. The next stage involves evaluating alternative options based on affordability, quality, and suitability. Finally, a purchase decision is made. Throughout this process, marketers have a crucial role in guiding and influencing consumers' decisions through tailored marketing strategies and communication.

Marketers need to differentiate their offerings from competitors in the highly competitive marketplace. By doing so, they can stand out and capture users' attention with commercial investigation intent. Various strategies can be employed to achieve this differentiation. One such approach is creating a unique selling proposition that highlights the unique benefits and features of the offering. Specialised features, competitive pricing, exceptional customer service, and innovative marketing campaigns can also help distinguish a product or service from others. Examining successful differentiation strategies companies implement across different industries can provide valuable insights and inspiration.

Customer reviews and testimonials play a significant role in commercial investigation intent. Potential customers value the opinions and experiences of others when making purchasing decisions. As marketers, we can leverage positive reviews and testimonials to build trust and credibility with potential customers. Effective strategies involve actively soliciting reviews, displaying them prominently on websites and marketing channels, and addressing any negative feedback constructively. By showcasing social proof, we can tap into its influence on transactional intent and increase conversions.

Marketers can create comparative content to guide users with commercial investigation intent towards their offerings. This type of content compares their offerings to competitors in a fair and informative manner. It provides potential customers with valuable insights and helps them make an informed decision. By highlighting their offerings' unique qualities and benefits, marketers can influence the purchasing decision and build brand loyalty. Creating comparative content requires a careful balance of objectivity and promotional messaging.

Social proof, such as user-generated content and influencer endorsements, wields significant power over commercial investigation intent. Potential customers are more likely to purchase when they see that others have had positive experiences. Marketers can utilise social proof to demonstrate their offerings' value, desirability, and trustworthiness. Marketers can differentiate their offerings by effectively showcasing social proof through user-generated content or influential endorsements and increasing the likelihood of conversions.

During the commercial investigation process, users may have various concerns and objections. Marketers need to anticipate and address these concerns proactively. Providing detailed product information, offering guarantees and warranties, and ensuring exceptional customer support are effective strategies for alleviating customer concerns. Proactive communication throughout the decision-making process is crucial in building trust and confidence. By addressing concerns head-on, marketers can help users overcome reservations and increase the likelihood of conversion.

In conclusion, commercial investigation intent is a critical aspect of the purchasing process that marketers must understand and leverage. Differentiation strategies, leveraging social proof, personalisation, addressing customer concerns, and creating persuasive calls-to-action are all essential components of intent-driven marketing. It is imperative for marketers to continually measure and analyse conversion success, study case studies and success stories, and adapt their strategies accordingly. Understanding and harnessing commercial investigation intent is the key to success in a constantly evolving marketplace.

Future Trends in User Intent

As the digital landscape evolves rapidly, marketers must stay ahead of the curve and adapt their strategies accordingly. In this subchapter, we explore emerging trends in user intent and delve into how marketers can navigate this dynamic landscape. By understanding users' evolving behaviours and motivations, marketers can tailor their strategies to meet their target audiences' ever-changing needs and expectations.

One of the most significant trends in user intent is the increasing popularity of voice search. With the advent of voice assistants like Siri, Alexa, and Google Assistant, more and more users are turning to their devices to perform searches. According to data from Techreport,[2] over 40 per cent of US adults surveyed in 2023 use voice search at least once a day and this is expected to rise.

The impact of voice search on user intent cannot be overstated. With traditional text-based searches, users typically enter short, concise queries into search engines. However, voice search changes the game by encouraging users to interact with search engines conversationally. This shift in behaviour has implications for marketers as it requires them to optimise their content to align with the conversational and long-tail keywords that users are likely to employ during voice searches.

To identify and target user intent in voice search queries, marketers can employ strategies such as analysing the types of questions users ask (predominantly via keyword research), monitoring voice search optimisation trends, and leveraging voice search analytics tools. By staying attuned to voice search users' specific nuances and preferences, marketers can ensure their content is optimised to meet the needs and expectations of this growing audience segment.

---

[2] See: https://techreport.com/statistics/voice-search-statistics/.

Another trend shaping user intent is the increasing sophistication of AI-powered assistants. Chatbots and virtual assistants equipped with artificial intelligence are becoming more adept at understanding and predicting user intent. These virtual entities gather and analyse user data, past interactions, and contextual information to deliver personalised experiences and assist users in achieving their goals.

For marketers, AI-powered assistants offer both opportunities and challenges. On the one hand, these assistants can enhance user experiences by providing personalised recommendations, guiding users throughout the decision-making process, and streamlining transactions. On the other hand, marketers must ensure that their strategies align with the capabilities and limitations of AI-powered assistants, optimising their content and interactions to provide a seamless experience for users interfacing with these virtual entities. I'm sure everyone reading this book will have had a negative experience with an AI-powered chatbot on a website or mobile device. Therefore, you are acutely aware of the kind of experience digital marketers should avoid to give potential customers a positive customer journey!

To successfully adapt marketing strategies for voice search and AI-powered assistants, marketers should prioritise several vital considerations. First and foremost, optimising content for natural language queries is paramount as users are more likely to employ conversational language when interacting with voice search. Additionally, providing concise and relevant answers to voice search queries is crucial as users expect immediate and accurate responses.

Personalisation and context awareness are also essential in meeting the evolving expectations of users. By tailoring experiences and recommendations based on user data and contextual information, marketers can create more meaningful connections and increase the likelihood of conversions.

In the realm of voice search and AI-powered assistants, data and analytics play a pivotal role in understanding user intent. Marketers can gain deep insights into user behaviour, preferences, and patterns by leveraging data. However, harnessing the power of data and analytics has its challenges. Marketers must navigate issues related to data privacy, data quality, and the ethical use of data. Additionally, it is crucial to constantly monitor and adapt data strategies to stay aligned with evolving privacy regulations.

Chapter 5

THE PSYCHOLOGY OF INTENT

Motivation and Intent

Motivation is the driving force behind human behaviour. It compels us to take action, make decisions, and shape our lives. Understanding the intricacies of motivation is not only fascinating from a psychological perspective, but it is also essential for creating effective marketing strategies that drive intent.

Motivation is a complex concept that encompasses a multitude of psychological factors. From an evolutionary standpoint, motivation can be traced back to our primal instincts for survival and reproduction. However, motivation extends far beyond these basic needs in the modern world. We are driven by many desires, ambitions, and aspirations that shape our motivations.

One widely recognised theory of motivation is Maslow's hierarchy of needs, which suggests that individuals have a hierarchy of needs that they strive to fulfil. These needs range from physiological needs like food and shelter at the bottom of the hierarchy to higher-level needs such as self-esteem and self-actualisation at the top of his hierarchy pyramid. If you've ever studied psychology, you'll know this theory and its limitations (a small sample size, qualitative research methods only, and the potential for researcher bias). However, it still raises interesting ideas about the range of factors that can influence our decision-making behaviours. By trying to understand these underlying psychological factors, we can gain valuable insights into consumer motivations and start to craft marketing messages that resonate with our target audiences.

Motivation plays a crucial role in the decision-making process. The level of motivation a person possesses can determine the actions they take and the choices they make. For instance, a highly motivated individual may be more prepared to engage in extensive information search and deliberation before purchasing. In contrast, someone with lower levels of motivation may make impulsive choices.

Marketers can leverage motivation to guide consumer choices by understanding the underlying motives that drive decision-making. By appealing to these motivations, whether the desire for status, belonging, wellbeing, or self-improvement—or more fundamental needs like food, clothing, and shelter—marketers can try to influence and shape consumer intent through effective targeting and messaging.

Motivation can be categorised into different types, including intrinsic and extrinsic motivation. Intrinsic motivation comes from within and is driven by personal enjoyment, curiosity, or a sense of accomplishment. On the other hand, extrinsic motivation is derived from external rewards or consequences, such as receiving a bonus or avoiding punishment.

Understanding the different types of motivation can help marketers tailor their messaging and appeals to align with their target audiences' specific desires and preferences. Marketers can develop strategies that tap into the right motivations and drive intent by identifying whether internal or external factors drive their customers.

Emotions are powerful catalysts for motivation. Our emotional state has a profound impact on our decision-making processes and can influence the actions we take. Marketers who can evoke specific emotions in their audiences can tap into their motivations and drive them towards a desired action.

Emotional appeals can range from evoking a sense of fear or urgency to inspire action to creating feelings of happiness or joy to associate with a product or brand. By understanding the emotional landscape of their target audiences and identifying the emotions that resonate most deeply, marketers can create campaigns that effectively tap into consumer motivation and propel intent.

Motivation can vary at different stages of the customer journey. As mentioned earlier, when I am talking about the customer journey, I am referring to several stages, starting with needs awareness (when individuals first decide they need a product or service or find out about a business), moving on to interaction with that brand—and others—as they evaluate their options before finalising their decisions and making purchases. The customer journey extends beyond post-purchase engagement (when customers seek help with their purchases, leave feedback, and ideally make other purchases), but in the context of this discussion into customer motivations, we focus only on the stages of decision-making up to purchase.

At the awareness stage of the customer journey, consumers may have low motivation and be unaware of their exact needs or desires. Marketers can engage and nurture consumers at this stage by providing valuable information and insight, sparking curiosity, and awakening latent desires.

Consumers' motivations typically increase through the consideration and decision stages. Marketers can leverage this increased motivation by providing compelling reasons to choose their products or services, highlighting the benefits and features that align with the customers' desires (as well as their unique challenges and goals), and reinforcing the urgency to take action.

Understanding and leveraging motivation is crucial for marketers in driving intent. To effectively tap into motivation, marketers should:

- Conduct thorough research to understand their target audiences' desires, needs, and motivations.
- Craft messages and appeals that resonate with the specific motivations of their audiences.
- Create experiences that fulfil consumer desires and align with their motivations.

- Use emotional appeals to tap into consumer motivation and create a strong connection with the brand or product.
- Tailor messaging and engagement strategies to align with the consumers' levels of motivation at different stages of the customer journey.

By harnessing the power of motivation, marketers can influence consumer behaviour, shape intent, and build long-lasting relationships with their customers.

Motivation is a fundamental driver of human behaviour and plays a pivotal role in shaping intent. By understanding the psychological factors that drive motivation, marketers can create effective strategies that align with consumer desires, tap into emotions, and guide them towards desired actions. Harnessing the power of motivation in marketing is a powerful tool for driving intent and establishing meaningful connections with consumers. In the following subchapter, we explore the topic of ethical marketing and the role it plays in shaping consumer intent.

Emotions and Intent

Emotions are a complex and integral part of human psychology, influencing our thoughts, behaviours, and decision-making processes. In this subchapter, we delve deep into the topic of emotions and intent, exploring the relationship between the two and examining how marketers can effectively tap into the power of emotions to shape consumer intent.

Emotions and intent are intrinsically intertwined, with emotions often serving as a driving force behind our decisions. When faced with a purchasing decision, our feelings can heavily influence how we weigh the available options and what ultimately drives our choices. Marketers have long recognised the power of emotions in decision-making and successfully harnessed it in their marketing campaigns.

For example, think about the last time you saw a heart-warming advertisement that left you feeling a sense of warmth and nostalgia. Christmas adverts are one example of marketing activities that play heavily into these emotions; loveable carnivorous plants and adventurous carrots are some recent examples from UK Christmas advertising! The emotional connection created in that moment likely influenced your intent to purchase the product or support the brand. Marketers can effectively shape consumer intent and drive action by understanding and tapping into the specific emotions that resonate with their target audiences.

Positive emotions such as joy, happiness, and inspiration can be compelling motivators that drive intent. When we experience positive emotions, our brains release dopamine, a neurotransmitter associated with pleasure and reward. This surge of dopamine can create a sense of anticipation and motivation, leading us to take actions aligned with those positive emotions.

Marketers can evoke positive emotions through various strategies such as creating compelling storytelling narratives, highlighting their products' benefits and transformative aspects, or showcasing experiences that resonate with their target audiences' desires. For example, a luxury holiday resort advertisement may focus on creating feelings of relaxation and serenity, enticing potential customers to book a trip and experience those positive emotions for themselves.

While positive emotions can be powerful motivators, negative emotions also play a significant role in shaping intent. Fear, urgency, and frustration are negative emotions that can drive action. When we experience negative emotions, our brains are wired to seek resolution and relief, often resulting in actions driven by a desire to alleviate those negative feelings.

Marketers can strategically evoke negative emotions to drive intent by creating a sense of urgency, highlighting potential negative consequences, or presenting a problem that their products or services can solve. For example, an advertisement for a security system may tap into the fear of burglary, presenting their products as the solution to alleviate that fear and provide peace of mind. Marketing activities from many charities focus on portraying the suffering of individuals experiencing famine, drought, and war. These aren't pleasant images, but the negative emotions they stimulate in viewers can prompt them to feel compassion and empathy and donate to support the charity.

Emotional triggers are specific stimuli that evoke emotional responses in individuals. These triggers can vary widely from person to person and can be influenced by personal experiences, cultural backgrounds, and individual values. As marketers, understanding and leveraging these emotional triggers can be powerful in shaping intent.

Emotional triggers can include nostalgia, social validation, desire for status or belonging, and the need for self-expression. By identifying the emotional triggers that resonate most strongly with their target audiences, marketers can tailor their messaging and appeals to tap into them, creating a deep emotional resonance that drives intent.

While evoking emotions can be a powerful tool in marketing, it is essential to consider the ethical implications of its use. Marketers must prioritise responsible and transparent practices when tapping into consumers' emotions and shaping intent. The wellbeing and autonomy of individuals should be respected, and manipulation or exploitation of emotions must be avoided.

Guidelines for the ethical use of emotions in marketing include ensuring that the emotional appeal aligns with the truth and integrity of the brand, respecting consumers' boundaries, avoiding manipulation or deception, and being transparent about the intent behind the emotional appeals. By adhering to these ethical considerations, marketers can build trust, cultivate long-lasting relationships, and create positive brand associations.

Cognitive Biases and Intent

I have always been fascinated by human psychology, how it influences our decision-making, and the concept of bias: internal preconceptions that influence how we think and feel about people, places, and things. You can present an advert or social media post to one hundred people, and you'll have one hundred different interpretations of that content since we all have different experiences, levels of education, belief systems, and so on. As a result, it's essential to be aware of cognitive biases when carrying out any form of online or offline marketing.

Cognitive biases are inherent biases in human thinking that can significantly impact one's intent. These biases result from the brain's effort to simplify the vast amount of information it receives, often leading to errors and deviations from rationality. This subchapter explores the fascinating world of cognitive biases and their impacts on intent.

One of the most prevalent cognitive biases is confirmation bias. This bias refers to the tendency to seek information confirming our beliefs or opinions while disregarding or downplaying contradictory evidence. In the context of marketing and intent, confirmation bias can significantly influence how consumers make purchasing decisions. As consumers, we often seek information that aligns with our preconceived notions about a product or brand, leading us to ignore or dismiss alternative options. Marketers can leverage confirmation bias by strategically presenting information that supports their products or brands and reinforcing consumers' existing beliefs, thus increasing the likelihood of intent to purchase.

Loss aversion is another cognitive bias that profoundly affects intent. This bias refers to the strong preference for avoiding losses over acquiring gains. In marketing, loss aversion can be harnessed by highlighting the potential negative consequences of not purchasing a product or service. By presenting the product or service as a solution to a problem or a means to avoid loss, marketers can tap into consumers' aversions to losing out and increase their intent to purchase. Various strategies can be employed to evoke loss aversion, such as creating compelling storytelling narratives, emphasising the benefits and transformative aspects of products, or showcasing experiences that resonate with consumers' desires. One popular example of harnessing loss aversion in a marketing strategy is by offering consumers their money back if they are not satisfied with a product, highlighting that they are not at risk of losing money if they decide the product or service isn't right for them after they have purchased it.

While positive emotions are often highlighted as motivators, negative emotions also significantly shape intent. Negative emotions like fear, urgency, and frustration trigger the brain's built-in mechanisms to seek resolution and relief. This drive to alleviate negative feelings can result in actions driven by a desire to ease the negative feelings users might be experiencing. Marketers can strategically tap into negative emotions to drive intent by creating a sense of urgency, highlighting potential negative consequences, or presenting a problem their product or service can solve. Marketers can effectively shape consumer intent and drive action by addressing these negative emotions head-on and providing a solution.

Social Influence and Intent

Individuals do not exist in a vacuum, unaffected and uninfluenced by the thoughts, experiences, and expectations of others around them. In this subchapter, we consider the issue of social influence and its connection to intent-driven marketing. We explore the relevance of social proof and influencers in shaping consumer behaviour and discuss how marketers can utilise these social dynamics to their advantage.

At its core, social proof refers to the tendency of individuals to look to others for guidance and validation when making decisions. In marketing, social proof plays a significant role in influencing user intent. By showcasing customer reviews, testimonials, and social media engagement, marketers can tap into the power of social proof to establish credibility and trust with their target audiences. When consumers see others affirming the value and quality of a product or service, the intent to purchase is strengthened. Through social proof, marketers can create a sense of legitimacy and build confidence in their offerings.

Today, the influence of online personalities, commonly known as influencers, cannot be underestimated. These individuals can shape user intent through their authenticity, expertise, and ability to connect with their audiences. There are different types of influencers, ranging from micro-influencers with niche audiences to macro-influencers with massive reach. Marketers can strategically partner with influencers whose values align with their brands and leverage their influence to shape consumer intent. By incorporating influencer endorsements into marketing campaigns, marketers can tap into the trust and credibility that influencers have established with their followers, further strengthening intent to purchase.

Trust is the cornerstone of any successful marketing strategy, and social influence plays a pivotal role in fostering trust in the minds of consumers. Authenticity and transparency are critical components of leveraging social influence for intent-driven marketing. As a result, marketers must partner with trustworthy influencers who embody the values of their brands and avoid deceptive tactics that erode trust. User-generated content can also be a powerful tool in building trust as it showcases real-life experiences and testimonials from satisfied customers. These are often individuals who fall within your target demographic and, therefore, share common characteristics—age, geographic location, brand preferences, and so on)—with potential customers. Marketers can establish a sense of trustworthiness and credibility that influences consumer intent by focusing on transparency and authenticity.

When crafting marketing content, it is essential to consider the role of social influence and create experiences that resonate with consumers' desires. Incorporating social proof, such as customer testimonials or expert endorsements, can significantly impact intent-driven marketing. Marketers can create a sense of social validation and establish credibility by showcasing individuals who have benefited from the product or service. Emotional appeals also effectively leverage social influence as they tap into the desires and aspirations of consumers. The power of storytelling, vivid imagery, and relatable narratives can evoke emotions that drive intent to purchase.

However, just because an influencer appears to fit in with your brand identity, ethos, and target demographic, it is crucial to monitor and analyse the impact of any social influence strategies that are adopted. Various tools are available to help you track social media metrics—including native statistics from the social media pages themselves—influencer reach, and engagement levels. By understanding these analytics, marketers can refine their strategies and identify the most effective tactics for influencing consumer intent. Tracking these metrics allows marketers to gain valuable insights into the success of their campaigns and make data-driven decisions that optimise their marketing efforts, putting more money into successful projects and diverting funds from unsuccessful partnerships.

Ethical Considerations in Influencing Intent

Ethical practices are of utmost importance in marketing as they shape consumer behaviour and contribute to the overall trust and credibility of brands. In this subchapter, I explore various topics related to ethical considerations in influencing intent, providing valuable insights and guidelines for marketers to navigate these complex issues.

In marketing, the power to manipulate consumer intent is a vital tool in shaping behaviour and driving sales. Marketers skilled at understanding consumer psychology and employing various strategies to influence intent often find the greatest success with their marketing activities. Through persuasive advertising, targeted messaging, or personalised recommendations, marketers can shape the desires and aspirations of consumers. However, this power comes with ethical implications. The manipulation of intent raises questions about the authenticity and honesty of marketing practices. As marketers, we must be mindful of the ethical issues that can arise from manipulating intent and strive to balance effective persuasion and responsible marketing.

When marketers manipulate intent, they potentially infringe upon consumer autonomy and the freedom to make informed choices. By using persuasive techniques, marketers can steer consumers towards making decisions they may not have otherwise made. This raises concerns about the justifiability of such practices and the limits of marketing influence. As marketers, we have an ethical responsibility to respect consumer autonomy and allow individuals to make decisions based on their values and preferences. Understanding the implications of intent manipulation on consumer autonomy is crucial when balancing influencing behaviour and upholding individual choice.

One of the core ethical dilemmas marketers face is influencing intent while maintaining honesty. Marketers need to be transparent and truthful in their practices as deceptive intent manipulation can lead to negative consequences, such as consumer distrust and damage to brand reputation. Marketers should strive to create marketing campaigns that are persuasive and grounded in honesty and integrity. By providing accurate information and setting realistic expectations, marketers can build trust with consumers and foster long-term relationships based on mutual respect.

To maintain ethical standards, marketers must avoid manipulative tactics that undermine consumer autonomy and free will. This requires an understanding of the line between persuasion and coercion. Marketers should prioritise empowering consumers through informed decision-making rather than exerting undue influence. Marketers can create an environment that respects consumer autonomy and fosters trust by ensuring consumers have access to all relevant information and providing opportunities for unbiased evaluation.

There are several other ethical considerations related to marketing that move away from the idea of influence but are essential to mention here. For example, obtaining informed consent from consumers to market to them via email, text message, and even retargeting is an ethical obligation for marketers, as well as something that ties in with data protection regulations like the General Data Protection Regulations (GDPR) and Privacy and Electronic Communication Regulations (PECR). Marketers enable consumers to make informed choices by providing concise and accurate information. Transparency is critical in ensuring that consumers are fully aware of the intentions and implications of marketing practices. Marketers should disclose potential conflicts of interest or affiliations with influencers and provide comprehensive information about the marketed products or services. Building trust through transparent marketing practices not only safeguards consumer rights but also contributes to the overall credibility and reputation of the industry.

Marketers must exercise heightened ethical considerations when targeting vulnerable populations such as children, older adults, or individuals with limited decision-making capacities. These populations may be more susceptible to manipulation and exploitation, making it crucial for marketers to adopt responsible and ethical targeting practices. Marketers should prioritise the wellbeing of these populations, avoiding tactics that could prey on their vulnerabilities. By employing safeguards and adhering to ethical guidelines, marketers can ensure their marketing efforts are inclusive, respectful, and protective of vulnerable individuals.

Ethical standards in marketing are constantly evolving. Marketers must stay updated with changing norms and regulations to ensure their practices align with societal expectations. Marketers can navigate the complex landscape of ethical considerations in influencing intent by actively engaging in ethical discussions, following industry best practices, and seeking guidance from regulatory authorities. Staying informed and adaptable is critical to maintaining ethical integrity in marketing practices.

Involving consumers in ethical marketing practices is essential to building trust and fostering meaningful connections. By seeking input from consumers and engaging them in decision-making processes, marketers can create marketing campaigns that align with their values and desires. Sending out customer questionnaires, carrying out interviews, and engaging with focus groups can help to build a picture of consumer attitudes towards a business's products, services, and marketing activities, helping a business to ensure that its marketing efforts are ethical, respectful, and relevant. By actively listening to consumer feedback and incorporating their perspectives, marketers can create marketing experiences that resonate with their target audiences and drive intent ethically and responsibly.

Chapter 6
INTENT-BASED KEYWORD RESEARCH

In this chapter, we delve into the crucial role that intent plays in keyword research, an activity that should be the cornerstone of any marketing activity for any business. Many people associate keyword research with paid advertisements in the search engine results pages or for SEO purposes. However, understanding what our potential customers are searching for, the language and terminology they use, and how many people are searching for those phrases can be valuable at all stages of a business's development. It can help start-ups determine the demand for their products and services, help companies understand consumer demand for their products or services, and help organisations understand what people want to know about the products and services they deliver and have meaningful conversations with them.

Keyword research is invaluable, but it's not static. Customer preferences and needs change, and the technology used when searching for information also changes. As a result, it's an activity that needs to be revisited regularly and can be fundamental to business success.

I could go on for days about the value of keyword research for business development. However, as this book's primary focus is search intent, we will return to the topics of paid advertising on search engines and organic SEO. By gaining insights into the motivations and desires of our target audiences, we can optimise our websites and content to meet their needs, thereby boosting search rankings and conversion rates. With this understanding, let us explore the depth of intent in keyword research and its potential impact on our success.

Before we discuss the impact of intent on keyword research, it is vital to establish what user intent entails. User intent is the underlying goal or purpose that drives an individual's search query. Keyword research is about understanding what users are trying to achieve when they enter specific keywords into search engines. As we have previously discussed, there are three main types of user intent: navigational, informational, and transactional.

Navigational intent typically arises when users are seeking a particular website or brand. Informational intent, on the other hand, occurs when users are seeking information, answers to their questions, or solutions to their problems. Transactional intent emerges when users are ready to purchase or take specific actions. Identifying and understanding these types of intent is essential as they dictate the appropriate keywords and content that should be targeted.

User intent plays a significant role in determining search visibility. Search engines like Google prioritise websites and content that align with user intent, ensuring that the most relevant results are displayed to users. When users conduct a search, search engine algorithms aim to satisfy their intent by presenting the most relevant websites in the SERPs. By targeting user intent, we increase our chances of ranking higher in the SERPs and gaining visibility to our ideal audience.

Understanding user intent also helps us optimise our websites for featured snippets, a coveted position at the top of the search results that provide concise, direct answers to user queries. By tailoring our content to address users' intentions and delivering the most valuable information, we increase our chances of securing featured snippets, further enhancing visibility and authority in the eyes of search engines.

Beyond search visibility, user intent has a profound impact on conversion rates. Conversion rates refer to the percentage of visitors who take a desired action, such as purchasing or filling out a contact form. By understanding user intent, we can create relevant and persuasive content that aligns with users' motivations, effectively guiding them through the customer journey and increasing the likelihood of conversion.

When we align content with user intent, we provide the information and solutions users seek. This builds trust and credibility and enhances the overall user experience. By addressing users' intentions and providing valuable content at each stage of their journeys, we can establish strong connections and influence their decision-making processes, ultimately driving higher conversion rates.

Now that we understand the significance of user intent in search visibility and conversion rates, it is crucial to incorporate this understanding into our keyword research strategies. Keyword research should no longer focus solely on identifying high-volume or highly competitive keywords. Instead, it should revolve around understanding the intent behind those keywords and selecting ones that align with our target audiences' motivations.

Thorough research is essential for understanding user intent. We must analyse search queries through tools like https://keywordstrategytool.com/ or other keyword research tools to gain insights into the language users use and the context in which they search. Additionally, competitor analysis can provide valuable information about how others in our industry are optimising for user intent, allowing us to uncover keywords or content gaps we can exploit.

One of the primary methods for uncovering user intent is through keyword analysis. By analysing search queries and identifying patterns in search intent, we can better understand what users are looking for and tailor content accordingly. This involves looking for keywords that indicate navigational, informational, or transactional intent. For example, 'buy', 'how to', and 'reviews' typically demonstrate transactional, informational, and navigational intent, respectively.

To identify user intent, we should pay close attention to the language users use, the specific questions they ask, and the type of content that currently ranks highly in the SERPs for those queries. By spotting patterns in the keywords and analysing search queries, we gain valuable insights into the intent driving users' searches, allowing us to create relevant and engaging content that meets their needs.

Understanding user intent enables us to make strategic keyword selection and optimisation decisions. By selecting keywords that align with user intent, we increase our chances of ranking higher in the SERPs and reaching our target audience effectively. Moreover, aligning content with user intent increases search visibility and enhances the overall user experience on our websites.

To optimise our chosen keywords for user intent, we should align various on-page elements such as title tags, meta descriptions, and headers with the intent behind the keywords. For example, if the intent behind a keyword is informational, we should create content that thoroughly answers the user's question and provides valuable insights. Ensuring that our content matches the intent behind the keywords ultimately contributes to higher search rankings and increased visibility.

Understanding user intent goes hand in hand with content creation and optimisation. By comprehending why users search for specific keywords, we can tailor content to address their intentions directly, providing them with the information or solutions they seek. This calls for creating valuable, engaging content that aligns with the user's journey and offers genuine value.

Optimising content for user intent involves including

relevant keywords in the content naturally while still ensuring a smooth reading experience. It requires incorporating long-tail keywords that reflect users' specific interests and needs. Furthermore, in-depth content that covers various aspects of a user's search query can increase engagement and time spent on our website, signalling to search engines that our content is valuable and should be ranked higher.

Tracking and measuring the impact of user intent on search rankings and conversion rates is imperative for evaluating the success of our keyword research strategies. Analytics tools such as Google Analytics and Google Search Console can provide valuable insights into the performance of our content, enabling us to monitor the influence of user intent on our search rankings and conversion rates.

By analysing data from these tools, we can identify patterns and trends that indicate the effectiveness of our user intent-based keyword research strategies. For example, we can assess which keywords and content drive the most traffic and conversions, enabling us to adjust our strategies if necessary. Continuous optimisation and adjustment based on user intent data will improve search rankings and increase conversion rates.

Tools and Techniques for Intent-Based Keyword Research

Now that we've discussed the significance of carefully considering consumer intent as you conduct keyword research for your business, it's worth revisiting the basics of practical keyword research. It's a concept that many are familiar with but few have invested time and effort into.

Keyword research is all about finding relevant and irrelevant search queries about your business's product or service that potential customers are typing into the search engines. So, what exactly is a relevant keyword? A relevant keyword is usually a word or phrase associated with your business—or the products or services you uniquely provide—that will likely be typed into the search engines by someone who wants to purchase that product/service or find out more information about it based on their user intentions. An example that I use a lot is that of a bed and breakfast in Aylesbury. Some people wrongly assume that 'bed', ' breakfast', and 'Aylesbury' are appropriate keywords, but these are too general. 'Bed' could be typed in the search engines to look for bed manufacturers, recommendations for duvet covers, tips on how to sleep soundly, or get rid of bedbugs. 'Breakfast' could be used to search for breakfast recipes, local cafés, or specialist crockery. (Melon baller, anyone?). And 'Aylesbury' could be typed into the search engines about the theatre, local walks, car park locations, information about the bus or train station in the town, and so on. (Fun fact: The bus station in Aylesbury was once named the most depressing place in the whole of the United Kingdom.), etc. To ensure that we target the right kinds of people, we need to be more specific and use the whole 'bed and breakfast' phrase to ensure that we only target people actively and explicitly searching for bed and breakfast accommodations. However, once again, the phrase 'bed and breakfast' is too general. People could be looking for accommodations in New Zealand, Canada, or anywhere in between! In the case of the bed and breakfast business in Aylesbury, it was necessary to be far more specific and look for keywords that were based on the phrase 'bed and breakfast Aylesbury'. For example:

- Bed and breakfast Aylesbury (260 UK searches per month)
- B&B Aylesbury (320 UK searches per month)
- Aylesbury Bed and Breakfast (210 UK searches per month)

Notice how we've used the ampersand rather than 'and' in some keyword ideas as these may have a monthly search volume, and we shifted the location from one end of the phrase to the other. You must be creative when thinking about how people might describe your business as it's not always obvious how people search for your business's products and services. It's also worth making notes of any industry-specific jargon you might use and consider what members of the general public (if they are your target customers) might use instead of that jargon to describe your products and services. For example, if you're in the plastic surgery business, consider the difference between the keywords 'nose job' (49,500 UK searches per month) and 'rhinoplasty' (135,000 UK searches per month) and consider which is most appropriate for your customers, or if a strategy targeting both would be more beneficial to your business.

In this era of voice-activated virtual assistant devices, it's also worth considering whether there are any questions that your potential customers might ask the search engine if they were looking for you. For example, 'Where is a good place to stay in Aylesbury?' could be an appropriate and highly relevant keyword phrase to focus on if further research shows that people are actively and specifically looking for that information.

Once you've come up with a selection of potential keywords that you think would be appropriate for your business, you then need to work out which options, if any, are actively searched for by your customers every month as some of your ideas may not have any monthly searches associated with them; some may have hundreds or thousands! This is where tools like https://keywordstrategytool.com/ are helpful. They allow you to quickly determine monthly search volumes and competition levels for your keyword ideas and then collate a selection of related keywords that you might not have thought about.

Another error people often make with keyword research is opting for keywords and phrases with huge monthly search volumes (in the tens of thousands!) thinking that it's a surefire way to drive more traffic to their websites. Unfortunately, this isn't always the case. For starters, keywords with thousands of monthly searches are often relatively generic. They may not be hugely accurate for your business, leading to the potential for increased traffic to a page but a high bounce rate (the number of people who leave the page after a matter of seconds without navigating further through the site), since most people landing on that page may quickly realise the content isn't exactly what they were looking for. It's worth noting that Google Analytics has now removed the bounce rate metric from its tool, opting instead for engagement rate, which describes the number of people actively engaging with the website and navigating through it. Some other tools, however, still use the bounce rate metric.

Another problem businesses face when targeting generic, popular keywords is that it's more likely they'll have competition from other companies for these more obvious keywords. Many of them may have been targeting the keyword for a long time and have a well-established position in the SERPs. As a result, it's unlikely that they'll rank positively for these high-value keywords for a long time—if ever! So if you're looking for a front-page listing in the SEPRs for your chosen keywords, you must be tactical! From experience, we recommend targeting keywords with under a thousand monthly searches (and more than no monthly searches, obviously) and with a medium competition level if you want to rank positively in a timely manner. It's not unusual to see businesses who have followed this methodology find themselves with a handful of relevant listings on the front page of Google, Yahoo, and Bing within eight to twelve weeks of starting the optimisation process, and for these businesses to see results continuing to improve over time with continued dedication to the methodology.

So why should you invest time and money into comprehensive keyword research? The reason is opportunity. Suppose you only find a few keywords or phrases related to your business. In that case, you may miss out on reaching those potential customers who describe your business/products/services using different words and phrases (including slang and jargon, as well as regular spelling mistakes) in the search query box. One practical example of a business missing key opportunities due to poor keyword research was a global fashion retailer that sold hooded sweatshirts and other casual clothing for men and women. Their previous keyword research activities had identified just 320 relevant keywords relating to 'hoodies', whereas we were able to identify over 9,436 relevant keywords relating to 'men's', 'women's', and 'unisex' hoodies). The complete list that our business was able to provide meant the organisation had a broader choice when selecting a relevant keyword for all their hoodies and had significantly more data that they could use in their paid-for advertising of hoodies and when writing about hoodies on social media and in their content marketing materials.

Unfortunately, comprehensive keyword research for a business is a time-consuming task. Even if you don't sell physical products, you likely offer your customers a range of services, and each of these can be described in more than one way. It's not unusual to generate 5,000 to 10,000 potentially relevant keyword suggestions for a business owner during comprehensive keyword research (with lists for some online shops reaching 100,000 keywords), highlighting the importance of investing time into this valuable marketing and business development activity.

Keyword	Monthly search volume (UK)	Cost Per Click	Competition Level (1 is high, 0 is low)	Number of searches March '24	Number of searches Feb. '24
Pub in Aylesbury	1900	£0.49	0.04	1900	1900
Best Pub in Aylesbury	140	£0 (not enough data)	0.02	210	140
Pub Accommodation Aylesbury	20	£0.30	0.15	10	20
Worst Pub in Aylesbury	0 (less than 10 per month)	£0	0	0	0

Figure 1. Example of data collated by https://keywordstrategytool.com/.

It's not just the keywords that are directly related to the products and services offered by a business that are important when it comes to SEO and pay-per-click (PPC) advertising on the SERPs. Phrases that are similar but irrelevant are also incredibly useful, particularly when it comes to keeping costs low with paid advertising on search engines.

Negative keywords are keywords that you wouldn't use to describe your products/services or business. They could contain the names of your competitors, geographic references outside of the area you service, or phrases that are too general or completely irrelevant. These words are still valuable and shouldn't be deleted as this information can be used in your paid-for advertising campaigns to ensure that your adverts don't show to anyone who types in any of these irrelevant keywords into the search engine. When carrying out keyword research, tools like https://keywordstrategytool.com/ will automatically collate all the phrases the search engine links with the products and services you deliver. If you were searching for keywords relating to cosmetic face masks, the type saturated with a serum that leaves your skin feeling fabulous, it's worth noting that keywords relating to medical and fabric face masks used to help reduce the spread of viruses would also appear in the results. In the case of cosmetic face masks, all keywords relating to virus-preventing face masks would be considered negative.

Once you have separated your keywords into positive and negative lists, you can start to break the list down further into phrases with navigational, informational, or transactional intent. Organising and categorising keywords based on user intent helps us understand users' different goals and motivations when searching for specific keywords. This categorisation allows marketers to create content that directly addresses user intentions and guides them through the customer journey. By providing the right information at the right stage of the users' journeys, marketers can establish strong connections and influence their decision-making process, ultimately driving higher conversion rates.

Once the keyword list is organised and categorised, refining and expanding it through ongoing monitoring and analysis are essential. User intent may change over time, and new keywords may emerge as trends and preferences shift. By regularly reviewing and updating the keyword list, marketers can stay relevant and optimise content for the evolving needs of their target audiences.

In conclusion, understanding user intent is crucial for effective keyword research and content optimisation. By utilising the tools and techniques discussed in this chapter, marketers can uncover user intent, generate a comprehensive list of keywords, and create content that aligns with user motivations. This approach enhances search visibility and rankings and increases conversion rates by providing users with the information and solutions they seek. In the following subchapter, we explore the intricacies of content optimisation and how it can further enhance the impact of user intent in our digital marketing efforts.

Long-Tail Keywords and Intent

Before further investigating the connection between long-tail keywords and user intent, it is crucial to define what long-tail keywords are. Long-tail keywords are more specific and less competitive than their broad-term, generic counterparts. They consist of longer phrases that more accurately reflect the specific intent of users. For example, while a generic keyword may be 'running shoes,' a long-tail keyword could be 'best lightweight running shoes for long-distance trail running.' The critical advantage of long-tail keywords lies in their ability to target a niche audience, allowing marketers to home in on users actively searching for specific products, information, or services.

To introduce the concept of long-tailed keywords further, let's think about cats. If I sell cat products (food, toys, hats, and so on), the majority of the keyword phrases that I would adopt to appeal to individuals with sales intent would be shorter, product-based keywords like cat food, which has 27,100 monthly UK searches, and cat raw food, which has 5,400 monthly UK searches. However, when carrying out comprehensive keyword research, we soon discover dozens of long-tailed keywords, including many questions, that are highly specific and have lower levels of competition and a lower monthly search volume. For example:

- 'Why are cats afraid of cucumbers?'—1,300 UK searches per month.
- 'Why do cats like earwax?'—260 UK searches per month.
- 'What do cats think about their owners?'—70 UK searches per month.

Although these aren't product-related keywords and instead demonstrate information-gathering user intent, they can still prove incredibly helpful to businesses as part of a broader content marketing strategy. If an individual wants to know why cats like earwax, there is a strong possibility that the individual has a cat and, therefore, falls within the target demographic for my cat product eCommerce business. They may not be in the market for new cat food, treats, or toys at present, but because we have answered a burning question that they had, we have started to build a positive relationship with that user which may prove helpful when they are in the market for cat products later.

Marketers must employ various tools and techniques to effectively leverage long-tail keywords for user intent analysis. These tools range from keyword research and analysis to website analytics and user behaviour-tracking tools. By utilising these resources, marketers can gain valuable insights into the intent behind user searches and behaviour. These insights are a foundation for content creation, ad development, and overall marketing strategies.

Once we have identified user intent through long-tail keyword analysis, the next step is to create relevant content that aligns with that intent. For content creators like myself, long-tail keywords act as a guiding light, providing ideas and inspiration for valuable blog posts, informative articles, and other forms of content. By addressing users' specific needs and interests, we capture their attention and establish ourselves as a trusted source of information.

One of the most significant advantages of long-tail keywords is their ability to target highly motivated users. These users are further along in the buying process and are more likely to convert. By aligning our marketing campaigns with their specific intents, we can maximise our chances of reaching these motivated users.

While long-tail keywords offer various advantages in terms of understanding specific user needs and preferences, they also come with their limitations. Keyword research and targeting can be challenging, and user intent is not always straightforward. This is mainly because no matter how objective we try to be, it is natural to be influenced by our own inherent biases and interpret phrases in a way that we are familiar with, making keyword analysis subjective. Though we can't escape this, being aware of this potential issue can prove beneficial in reducing the impact of researcher bias on our investigations into user intent.

Adapting Keyword Research to Changing Intent

User intent isn't static; it constantly evolves and varies over time and across markets. As a digital marketer, it is essential to recognise this ever-changing nature of user intent. For example, user intent may shift towards gift-buying or event planning during holidays or seasonal events. Additionally, different markets may have unique nuances in user intent, requiring marketers to adapt their keyword research accordingly. However, keeping up with these changes can be challenging as marketers constantly battle to stay relevant and understand the shifting landscape of user intent.

Adapting keyword research to changing intent is necessary to remain competitive and relevant in the market. Outdated keyword research can lead to irrelevance as it fails to capture the evolving intentions of users. Marketers can optimise their content, advertisements, and overall marketing strategies to meet user needs by staying current with user intent. This alignment enhances the user experience, increases the likelihood of conversions, and improves overall results.

- **Strategy 1: Monitoring Market Trends**
  Monitoring market trends is a crucial strategy to understand changing user intent. Marketers can gain valuable insights into their target audiences' evolving needs and desires by tracking shifts in user behaviours and preferences. Tools and techniques such as social listening, trend analysis, and web analytics can provide valuable data on user intent. With this information, marketers can update their keyword research strategies accordingly, ensuring they target relevant keywords that align with user intent.

- **Strategy 2: Analysing Competitor Keyword Strategies**
  Analysing competitor keyword strategies is another valuable strategy for adapting keyword research to changing intent. By examining the keywords that competitors are targeting, marketers can

gain insights into the interests and intentions of their target audiences. This analysis allows them to adjust their keyword research and stay ahead of the competition in capturing users' attention. Tools and techniques such as competitor analysis tools, website audits, and keyword gap analysis can aid in identifying competitor keyword strategies and leveraging this information to adapt keyword research.

- **Strategy 3: Conducting Regular Keyword Research**

  Regular keyword research is a fundamental strategy in adapting to changing user intent. Marketers can identify new trends, emerging topics, and shifting user needs by conducting ongoing keyword research. This process involves utilising keyword research tools like https://keywordstrategytool.com/, exploring related search queries, and monitoring changes in search engine algorithms. By implementing a routine of regular keyword research, marketers can stay informed and proactive in adapting their keyword strategies to match evolving user intent.

- **Strategy 4: Using Long-tail Keywords**

  Long-tail keywords are crucial in aligning keyword research with specific user intent. These keywords, which are longer and more specific than broad terms, help target niche markets and capture highly relevant traffic. By incorporating long-tail keywords into keyword research, marketers can reach users with higher intents to purchase or engage with their content. Identifying and incorporating long-tail keywords involves utilising keyword research tools, conducting competitor analysis, and leveraging user-generated content and feedback.

- **Strategy 5: Leveraging User-Generated Content and Feedback**

  User-generated content and feedback are a gold mine for providing insights into user intent. By analysing user comments, reviews, and feedback, marketers can better understand their target audiences' intentions, desires, and pain points. This information can then be used to align keyword research with user intent, creating content that addresses their specific needs. Various tools and strategies, such as social listening, surveys, and sentiment analysis, can aid in gathering and analysing user-generated content and feedback.

- **Strategy 6: Testing and Optimising Keyword Performance**

  Testing and optimisation are vital components of adapting keyword research to changing intent. By testing different keyword strategies, marketers can measure and analyse the performance of keywords in driving traffic, engagement, and conversions. This process involves utilising A/B testing, conducting keyword performance analysis, and leveraging tools like Google Analytics. Based on test results, marketers can optimise their keyword strategies to align with user intent, ensuring maximum impact and effectiveness.

- **Strategy 7: Collaborating with Other Teams for Insights**
  Collaborating with other teams within the organisation can provide valuable insights into changing user intent. Teams such as sales, customer service, and product development can offer unique perspectives on customer needs and desires. Marketers can access valuable data and insights that inform keyword research and ensure relevance in their marketing strategies by engaging in cross-functional collaboration. Regular meetings, feedback loops, and shared data platforms can facilitate effective collaboration and knowledge sharing.

As well as pre-existing data-gathering tools for keyword research, technological advancements in Natural Language Processing (NLP), machine learning, and AI can help with keyword research and determining the consumer intent behind different keyword search phrases.

Natural Language Processing (NLP) and Keyword Analysis

Natural Language Processing (NLP) is a field of study focusing on the interaction between computers and human language. It involves the development of algorithms and techniques that enable machines to understand and interpret natural language, allowing them to process and analyse text in a way that mimics human comprehension. NLP plays a crucial role in search-intent analysis by providing insights into the underlying meaning and context of search queries.

NLP techniques go beyond basic keyword matching when attempting to understand search queries. They enable machines to dissect the structure of a query, identify keywords and phrases, and decipher the underlying intent behind the search. By analysing patterns, sentiments, and named entities within the query, NLP algorithms can extract meaningful information that helps to categorise and classify user intent.

The benefits of using NLP techniques in search-intent analysis are numerous. Firstly, NLP enhances the accuracy and precision of understanding user intent, resulting in more relevant search results. Search engines can provide more tailored recommendations and personalised content by discerning a user's true purpose behind a search query. Additionally, NLP techniques improve user experience by ensuring search results align with their needs and expectations.

However, it is essential to acknowledge the limitations

and challenges of NLP in search-intent analysis. Language can be highly ambiguous, and context plays a significant role in determining the true intent behind a query. NLP algorithms must constantly adapt and evolve to keep up with the evolving nuances and language usage. Language-specific challenges such as slang, idioms, and specific cultural references can further complicate accurate intent classification.

Various NLP techniques are employed for user intent classification. Sentiment analysis, for example, helps determine the emotional tone of a query and can be utilised to identify whether a user is seeking positive or negative information. Named entity recognition is used to identify and extract specific entities such as names, locations, or organisations, aiding in understanding the context of the query. Topic modelling techniques help categorise queries into specific topics, providing a deeper understanding of user preferences and interests.

In the age of AI, NLP plays a vital role in understanding user intent for personalised searches. By leveraging NLP capabilities, search engines can analyse a user's search history, browsing behaviour, and contextual cues to gain insights into their preferences and deliver tailored search results. Understanding user intent at a deeper level allows for a more curated and personalised online experience, ultimately increasing user satisfaction and engagement.

It's important to note that challenges persist in NLP-based search-intent analysis. Data quality and quantity can affect the accuracy of NLP models. The lack of labelled training data for specific domains or industries can hinder accurate intent classification. Additionally, the rapid pace of language evolution and the need for domain-specific models pose continuous challenges that must be addressed through ongoing research and development.

The field of Natural Language Processing (NLP) is constantly evolving. With advancements in technology, new techniques and methods emerge that are revolutionising search-intent analysis. Deep neural networks, with the ability to model complex relationships and patterns, have shown great promise in capturing the intricacies of human language.

As we continue to explore the potential of NLP in search-intent analysis, it is crucial to consider the ethical implications of using these technologies. Privacy and data protection must be prioritised, and biases in data or models must be addressed to ensure fair and unbiased analysis. Responsible and ethical use of NLP in search-intent analysis requires transparency, accountability, and a commitment to balancing the benefits of these technologies while safeguarding user rights.

Natural Language Processing is a powerful tool in search-intent analysis, allowing machines to understand and interpret human language. By employing NLP techniques, search engines can gain deeper insights into user intent and provide more tailored and relevant search results. However, challenges and ethical considerations must be addressed to ensure the responsible implementation of NLP in the age of AI. As we continue developing and refining NLP technologies, the potential for understanding user intent and optimising search experiences expands, promising a future where search results align with user needs.

Chapter 7
INTENT-DRIVEN CONTENT MARKETING

Content Strategy and User Intent

In our online world, with an abundance of information available in our pockets and a reduction in attention spans, creating and delivering high-quality content that meets the needs and desires of users is more important and more challenging than ever.

As previously discussed, user intent is the underlying motivation or purpose behind a user's online search or engagement with content. Understanding user intent allows us to effectively create relevant and valuable content that meets their needs. By aligning a content strategy with user intent, we can optimise user experiences, drive engagement, and ultimately achieve marketing goals. This alignment allows businesses to connect with our target audience and build meaningful relationships. So how can we develop content that truly meets the needs of our target demographic?

- **Step 1: User research and analysis**
  A solid foundation of user research and analysis is crucial to develop intent-driven content plans. This framework involves conducting thorough research

to understand the target audience's desires, pain points, and motivations. We can gain valuable insights into user intent by employing surveys and interviews and analysing user behaviour data. Additionally, keyword research and social listening tools can help us identify trends and understand what users search for.

- **Step 2: Mapping user intent to content strategy**
  Once we have a deeper understanding of user intent, the next step is to map it to our content strategy. This framework involves identifying and prioritising user intentions and aligning them with the appropriate content topics and formats. By creating a comprehensive content mapping strategy, we can ensure that our content effectively addresses user needs at each stage of the customer journey, from needs awareness to post-purchase. This approach allows us to proactively alleviate their pain points, creating a seamless user experience.

- **Step 3: Content creation and optimisation**
  Creating content that meets user intent goes beyond simply providing information. It requires us to be strategic and consider how we can add value to their lives. This framework involves crafting content that is valuable, engaging, and tailored to user intent. By optimising our content with relevant keywords, incorporating multimedia elements, and

enhancing readability, we can further improve the user experience. Effective content creation and optimisation ensure that our content remains engaging while delivering on user expectations.

- **Step 4: Measurement and analysis**
  Measuring and analysing the performance of our intent-driven content is vital to understanding its impact on user intent. This step involves tracking key metrics, such as conversion and engagement rates, to assess the success of our content strategy. Utilising tools such as Google Analytics can provide valuable insights into user behaviour and allow us to iterate and refine our content plans. By staying attuned to these metrics, we can adapt our approaches and make data-driven decisions to continually meet user intent.

Optimising Content for Different Intent Types

Optimising content for different user intent types is a crucial aspect of digital marketing. We can effectively engage our audiences and guide them towards their desired actions by optimising content for informational, transactional, navigational, commercial investigation, and local intent.

The first type of user intent we need to address is informational intent. This intent revolves around users seeking information about a specific topic or query. They are looking for in-depth knowledge, detailed explanations, and reliable sources that can provide them with comprehensive information. Queries that fall under this category often start with 'how to', 'what is', or 'why', indicating a primary desire for knowledge. Understanding informational intent is crucial for structuring content to meet users' needs and expectations.

We must provide valuable and comprehensive information when structuring content for users with informational intent. Generic and surface-level content is unlikely to satisfy users' needs, so it is essential to go beyond the basics and offer detailed explanations, statistics, examples, and case studies. By delving into the details and presenting well-researched content, we establish our authority and position ourselves as a trusted resource in the industry.

In addition to offering valuable information, it is essential to structure content in a way that is easy to navigate and understand. Clear headings and subheadings help users find the specific information they seek, facilitating their journeys through our content. By organising our content effectively, we enable users to consume information in bite-sized chunks, making it more digestible and engaging.

Transactional intent is the second type of user intent we need to address. This intent is characterised by users who are ready to make a purchase or take a specific action. Users with transactional intent use queries that contain action-oriented terms such as 'buy', 'order', or 'download'.

To optimise content for transactional intent, we must incorporate persuasive elements that drive conversions and guide users towards their desired actions.

To effectively incorporate persuasive elements into content, we need to use compelling CTAs that clearly articulate the desired action, encouraging users to take that step. Our language should be persuasive and assertive, instilling a sense of urgency and importance. Social proof, such as customer testimonials or reviews, can also be leveraged to build trust and confidence, further driving conversion.

Navigational intent is a third type of user intent we must consider when optimising our content. Users with navigational intent seek specific websites or resources. Their queries often include brand names, website URLs, or specific terms related to the resources they seek. To meet the needs of users with navigational intent, we must structure our content to provide easy navigation and quick access to the desired information.

To ensure easy navigation for users with navigational intent, it is essential to have clear menus, site maps, and search functionality. By providing these tools, users can quickly find the information or resources they seek, ultimately enhancing their user experiences. A well-organised and easily accessible website satisfies user intent, increases user satisfaction, and encourages them to engage further.

The fourth type of user intent to consider is commercial investigation intent. Users with commercial investigation intent are in the process of researching and evaluating potential purchases. Their queries often include terms such as 'best', 'reviews', or 'comparison'. To optimise content for users with commercial investigation intent, we need to create content that supports them in their decision-making process.

We can use strategies such as comparison tables, customer testimonials, and product demonstrations to create content that supports users with commercial investigation intent. Comparison tables help users evaluate different options and make informed choices. Customer testimonials provide social proof and reassurance, building trust and confidence. Product demonstrations can give users a visual understanding of how a product or service works, helping them make confident purchase decisions. By providing content that supports users in their commercial investigations, we increase the chances of converting them into customers.

Finally, it's worth considering how to tailor content marketing activities for local intent. Users with local intent have specific geographical needs and expectations. Local intent revolves around users looking for products or services in their local areas. Their queries often include location-specific terms or phrases such as 'near me' or 'in [location]'. Optimising content for local intent requires a unique set of strategies and considerations.

To effectively localise content for users with local intent, it is crucial to include relevant location-based keywords. This ensures that our content appears in search results when users seek local options. Additionally, incorporating local reviews and testimonials helps establish user trust and credibility. Optimising content for local search results also plays a significant role in satisfying user intent as it ensures that our content is visible and accessible to the local audience. Ensuring that the business's listing on Google Business Profiles, for example, is up to date can help appeal to users with localised search intent.

It is important to note that intent optimisation works hand in hand with SEO. Understanding user intent can guide our keyword selections and content creation strategies. By aligning our content with user intent, we improve the user experience, increase engagement, and enhance our search engine rankings. Integrating intent optimisation with SEO is crucial in driving organic traffic and effectively reaching our target audience.

Once you've identified user intent and tailored your content marketing activities to effectively engage with the intentions of these users, you can't rest on your laurels. Continuous testing and refinement are essential when optimising content for different user intent types. User behaviour, conversion rates, and analytics provide valuable insights into how our content performs and whether it effectively meets user intent. By analysing this data, we can continually make data-driven adjustments and improvements to optimise the content's performance. This iterative process ensures we consistently create valuable and engaging content that satisfies user intent.

Measuring Content Success Based on Intent

Measuring content success based on intent allows us to refine our digital marketing strategies and deliver better results. In this subchapter, we explore the metrics and KPIs that can be used to measure the success of intent-driven content marketing campaigns.

Metrics and KPIs are the compasses that guide marketers through the vast ocean of digital content. Without these navigational tools, we would be floating aimlessly (sunburnt and hangry), with no way to evaluate the effectiveness of our efforts and find the way to our destination. Metrics and KPIs provide actionable insights into user behaviour and intent, helping us make data-driven decisions to optimise our content strategies.

Key metrics can provide valuable insights when measuring content success based on intent. One such metric is engagement rate. Engagement rate captures how users interact with our content, whether through likes, comments, shares, or other forms of engagement. By calculating the engagement rate, we can gauge the level of interest and intent our content generates. A higher engagement rate suggests that our content resonates with users and encourages them to act.

Conversion rate is another vital metric for measuring content success based on intent. It indicates the percentage of users who complete a desired action, such as purchasing or submitting a form. The conversion rate provides insights into the effectiveness of our content in driving user actions and achieving our intended goals. By analysing the conversion rate, we can identify areas for improvement and optimise our content to drive better results.

In addition to engagement and conversion rates, some other metrics and KPIs can provide valuable insights into content success based on intent. Metrics such as time on the page, scroll depth, and click-through rate can give further insight into user intent and engagement. These metrics help us refine our strategies and create content that aligns with user expectations.

Measuring content success based on intent allows us to refine our content marketing strategies. We can gain insights into user intent and preferences by analysing the metrics and KPIs discussed in this subchapter. These insights enable us to optimise our content, create engaging experiences, and drive better results. Through continuous analysis and refinement, we can adapt our strategies to meet the ever-changing landscape of user intent.

Measuring content success based on intent comes with its own set of challenges and considerations. Attribution of traffic, data accuracy (particularly in the age of privacy and electronic communication regulations, or PECR, where not all users can be tracked via cookies), and the need for ongoing measurement and analysis are just a few of the obstacles marketers face when trying to evaluate the success of their efforts. Accurately measuring intent-driven content success requires a holistic approach, incorporating multiple data sources and staying abreast of the latest analytical tools and techniques, and we need to continuously evolve and adapt our measurement strategies to ensure accurate and reliable results.

Chapter 8
INTENT AND SEO

The Role of Intent in SEO

Gone are the days when simply stuffing keywords into website content would guarantee a high ranking on SERPs. Today, search engines are becoming more sophisticated in their abilities to interpret user intent, and as a result, marketers must adapt their strategies to align with this powerful force.

Observing how search engines can now interpret user intent by analysing search queries, user behaviour, and contextual clues is fascinating. With the help of machine learning and NLP, search engines can determine what a user is searching for and why they are searching for it. By examining the language used in the search query and considering the user's previous behaviour, search engines can provide more accurate and relevant search results to satisfy the user's intent. This shift has transformed how marketers approach SEO. They now need to focus more on creating content that aligns with user intent rather than just targeting specific keywords.

Aligning website content with user intent is vital for

SEO success. By understanding user intent, marketers can create and optimise relevant and valuable content for users. This satisfies user needs and drives organic traffic to the website. Gone are the days of focusing solely on keyword optimisation; now, the focus must be on providing content that matches what users seek at a deeper level. By delivering value and addressing user intent, marketers can increase the visibility and credibility of their websites.

User experience plays a pivotal role in aligning with user intent. A user-friendly website design, straightforward navigation, and relevant internal linking are essential aspects that enhance the overall user experience. When users can easily navigate through a website and find the information they seek, it aligns with their intent and improves their overall satisfaction. Marketers should focus on creating intuitive website designs and clear pathways for users, ensuring that the website structure complements user intent and facilitates a seamless browsing experience.

In today's visually driven world, incorporating multimedia content has become increasingly critical. Marketers can provide a more engaging and informative user experience by integrating relevant images, videos, and infographics. Visual content can captivate users, communicate complex information effectively, and align with their intent. Including multimedia content enhances the overall user experience and increases the chances of users staying on the website longer, resulting in improved SEO performance.

The importance of mobile optimisation also cannot be overstated when attempting to align with user intent. With the exponential growth of mobile devices for online search, having a responsive website design and mobile-friendly content is essential. Mobile users have unique needs and behaviours, and websites that are not optimised for mobile will fail to align with their intent, resulting in low engagement rates and lost opportunities. By ensuring that websites are mobile-friendly and provide a seamless experience across devices, marketers can cater to the increasing number of mobile users and align their content with user intent.

As the world of SEO continues to evolve, the future of user intent looks promising. Emerging trends and technologies, such as voice search and artificial intelligence, are expected to further influence how search engines interpret and satisfy user intent. With its NLP capabilities, voice search requires search engines to understand intent more accurately and deliver voice-optimised search results. The rise of AI in search engines also enables more personalised and dynamic search experiences in which results can be tailored to individual user profiles and behaviours. As these technologies advance, marketers must stay on top of the latest developments and adapt their strategies to meet the ever-changing landscape of user intent in SEO.

On-Page Optimisation for SEO and User Intent

Creating content tailored to user intent is just one aspect of getting a website listed highly in the SERPs. The exact algorithms search engines use to determine the positions of websites in the SERPs are a mystery to all but those involved in their creation. Still, these algorithms likely consider hundreds of factors. However, despite the mysteries associated with the inner workings of search engines, there are widely accepted activities that can be adopted to help enhance a website's position in the SERPs. Following is a brief guide.

SEO refers to how pages on a website are gently manipulated to help them appear more visible to search engines for specific keywords. From my professional experience of working in SEO, I have found that it helps when a relevant keyword is used in the following six places on a webpage:

- *The webpage's URL slug* (that is, https://www ... insert-keyword-here.com). This may only be appropriate if you set up a new website or can easily name pages. Changing an existing URL to incorporate the keyword is possible, but it can lead to issues with 404 errors (an error that occurs when a webpage can't be found at a specific address) if other pages or posts link to the previous URL and aren't updated or a 301 redirect isn't established. If in doubt, seek help from your web developer.

- *The title of the page.* This should be between sixty-five and seventy characters long and contain the keyword. If you go over the prescribed number of characters, the extra letters will appear as ' ... ' in the search engine listings, so if you've got something important to say in the title, make sure it's within the character limit.

- *The content on the page.* This should contain between three hundred and five hundred words. The keyword should appear within the first one hundred characters. If you can mention the keyword naturally on the page two or three more times without the content coming across as 'spammy', that can help.

- *In the meta-description or snippet.* This should be between 150 and 160 characters long and should contain the keyword. Snippets are the adverts to your customers that appear in the SERPs, so make sure they are eye-catching and relevant to your business. As with the title on the page, if you go beyond the prescribed number of characters, the extra letters will appear as ' ... ' in the search engine listings, so use your character allocation wisely.

- *As a meta-keyword.* Please note that although some search engines claim to no longer recognise or use meta-keywords, alternative search engines may utilise this feature, so I recommend assigning your chosen keyword as a meta-keyword anyway. Remember that Google doesn't account for 100 per cent of the global search volume. Bing, Yahoo, and so on are also widely used. As a result, if you don't use meta-keywords, you could be putting yourself at a disadvantage.

- *In the alt-tag for one picture on the page.* Every page needs an image, and the alt-tag needs to feature the chosen keyword/phrase for the page. This needs to be done as search engine robots can't read images and need to know that a picture is relevant to any visitor to the page. This also helps make your site more accessible to individuals who use page-reader tools, so it is a great thing to do regardless of your SEO activities.

It's worth mentioning that including your business name in any of those places is unnecessary. If someone already knows your business name, they should be able to find you relatively simply by typing your business name into the search engine. Using your business name in the meta-description, title on the page, and so on, only removes valuable characters that you could use to help promote your business, products, and services more effectively to an audience of individuals who want your products or services and aren't already familiar with your business name.

As well as incorporating your chosen keyword in the places mentioned previously, it's also worth trying to incorporate an internal link on every page to help keep the search engine robots on your website for as long as possible. Your website won't necessarily be crawled and relisted by the search engines daily or even weekly, so when they visit the website, it's worth encouraging them to visit as much of the site as possible. If you can refer someone to another page (that is, by saying something like, 'If you'd like more information, get in touch!' and adding a link to the contact page) using an internal link, it's essential to make sure that your hyperlink text doesn't say 'Click here' or 'Read more' but uses the chosen keyword for the page you are directing towards to help show the robots that the content you are sending them to is relevant and optimised. If you can incorporate a link on each page, try adding it close to the bottom of the content so that the search engine robots can work through all the important information required to index a webpage before moving to the next page.

If you are optimising a website, it can take up to an hour to make all the recommended adjustments to the webpage, particularly if you struggle a little with content or aren't familiar with the back end of your website. The results aren't instant either as the search engine's robots may not pass your website again for days or weeks! As a result, it's worth submitting your sitemap to the search engine's search console or webmaster tools feature after a day of activity on the site to encourage the robots to return and ensure they can see all the pages you want them to index. If you use WordPress and have the Yoast plugin, this can help you locate your sitemap URLs, which can then be dropped into search console/webmaster tools to encourage reindexing.

How Does SEO Tie in with User Intent?

Meta tags, those behind-the-scenes snippets of HTML code, are often overlooked but play a vital role in conveying the purpose and relevance of a webpage to both search engines and users. By optimising meta tags to align with user intent, marketers can significantly improve search rankings and click-through rates. Crafting compelling titles and meta descriptions that accurately reflect the content of a webpage is crucial in capturing users' attention and enticing them to visit the website.

Headings, the hierarchically structured elements that guide users and search engines through the content of a webpage, are another crucial aspect of on-page optimisation. By optimising headings to align with user intent, marketers can enhance the user experience and elevate search rankings. Ensuring that headings accurately reflect the following content and entice users to delve deeper into the webpage is essential for navigation and SEO purposes.

Content, the heart and soul of any webpage, holds immense power in driving user engagement and search rankings. Marketers can establish their authority and resonate with their target audiences by creating valuable and relevant content that aligns with user intent. Understanding the needs and desires of users and optimising content to address those intents is the secret sauce that leads to improved search rankings and user engagement.

Incorporating relevant and optimised images and multimedia is paramount when aligning content with user intent. Visual elements have the power to captivate users, communicate complex information effectively, and enhance the overall user experience. From carefully selected images to engaging videos and interactive infographics, optimising multimedia content can significantly improve search rankings and user engagement.

Internal linking, the art of connecting webpages within a website, is vital in guiding users and search engines to relevant information. Marketers can enhance navigation and improve search rankings by incorporating relevant internal links that align with user intent. Connecting related content and providing clear pathways for users ensure a seamless browsing experience and keep users engaged with the website.

Technical SEO and User Intent

Technical SEO is another core component of a successful digital marketing strategy. It involves optimising a website's technical elements to improve its visibility and performance in SERPs. Website speed, mobile optimisation, and structured data implementation directly impact a user's experience and can influence whether or not they have a positive enough knowledge of the site to encourage the decision to make a purchase. A website that loads quickly, is mobile friendly, and provides structured information will create a seamless user experience and increase the likelihood of meeting user intent.

Website speed plays a vital role in fulfilling user intent. Since we are used to having access to the World Wide Web in our pockets, wherever and whenever we need it, users have become increasingly impatient. Slow-loading websites frustrate users, often leading to low engagement rates and diminished user satisfaction. When users search for information or products, they expect instant results. As a result, optimising website speed is crucial for meeting user intent and retaining users.

By improving website speed, marketers enhance the user experience and increase the likelihood of conversions. In 2017, research by Akamai Technologies Inc.[3] found that a one-second delay in page loading time can negatively impact conversion rates, reducing them by up to 7 per cent (Akamai, 2017). Therefore, continuously monitoring and optimising website speed are important to ensure it aligns with user expectations and fulfils their intent. Optimising website speed can involve minimising server response

---

[3] Akamai Online Retail Performance Report | Akamai (2017). Akamai.com. Available at: https://www.akamai.com/newsroom/press-release/akamai-releases-spring-2017-state-of-online-retail-performance-report.

time, compressing and optimising images, and leveraging browser caching. By reducing page load time, marketers can provide a seamless user experience and increase the chances of fulfilling user intent.

As previously mentioned, the proliferation of mobile devices has revolutionised how users access the internet. More and more users rely on their smartphones and tablets to browse the Web, making mobile optimisation a crucial aspect of meeting user intent. Ignoring mobile optimisation can result in a frustrating user experience, damaging the chances of fulfilling user intent and driving conversions. Responsive design and mobile-friendly interfaces are essential for meeting user intent on mobile devices. Ensuring that websites adapt seamlessly to different screen sizes and load quickly on mobile devices is paramount. Marketers must prioritise mobile optimisation and cater to the preferences and behaviours of mobile users. Doing so increases the chances of satisfying user intent and capturing their attention in a mobile-dominated era.

User Experience and Intent

User experience (UX) is at the heart of digital marketing. UX encompasses all aspects of a user's interaction with a business, product, or service. It goes beyond functional usability and accessibility to include visual design, content, and overall satisfaction. A positive user experience is essential in meeting user intent and achieving desired outcomes.

Aligning user experience with user intent is critical to providing relevant and meaningful experiences. By understanding what users want to accomplish, we can design experiences that cater to their needs and aspirations. For example, suppose we know that a customer has clear purchase intentions. In that case, we need to ensure that the CTA buttons to add products to the cart and checkout are clear and straightforward and that the payment process is quick and easy by providing guest checkout options, incorporating various payment methods, and so on. When users have a positive experience, it becomes easier for them to achieve their goals. A well-designed user experience can enhance user intent and increase motivation by guiding users towards their objectives and removing any obstacles to their journeys.

To drive higher engagement, it is essential to optimise the user experience. Intuitive navigation, clear CTAs, and responsive design are crucial strategies for enhancing user experience and increasing engagement. Personalisation and customisation also play significant roles in creating a user experience that resonates with individuals, capturing their attention and keeping them engaged. In addition, user feedback and continuous improvement can prove valuable in fine-tuning the user experience for higher conversion rates.

Fundamental design principles guide the creation of user experiences that meet user intent. Simplicity, consistency, and clarity are paramount in interface design. Visual hierarchy, information architecture, and content organisation are critical in guiding users towards their intended goals. These principles ensure that every interaction with a product or service is meaningful and purposeful.

The role of content cannot be overlooked when it comes to user experience and intent. Relevant and valuable content is instrumental in providing a meaningful user experience. A well-crafted content strategy and effective copywriting ensure the content aligns with user intent. By providing the right information at the right time, we can engage users and drive successful outcomes.

Chapter 9
INTENT-BASED PAID ADVERTISING

Understanding Intent Signals in Paid Advertising

Intent signals are the breadcrumbs left behind by users as they navigate the vast digital landscape. Huge quantities of data are generated by every digital channel that provides valuable insights into customer preferences, interests, and needs, helping marketers tailor their advertising campaigns to the right audience. These signals are crucial in the age of information overload, where the key to success lies in delivering the right message to the right people at the right time.

To truly harness the power of intent signals, it is essential to understand the types of signals that exist. As we have already discussed, search queries are one data source and offer a window into users' minds, revealing their purchasing intentions and desires. Other signals, such as website visits, content consumption, social media engagement, and previous purchase behaviour, can all be insightful indicators of intent.

Intent signals play a crucial role in ad quality and relevance. Understanding user intent allows marketers to create highly targeted, personalised ads that resonate with their audiences. With improved ad relevance comes higher quality scores, resulting in better ad placement and reduced costs. By aligning their messaging with the intent signals of their audience, marketers can unlock the true potential of their paid advertising campaigns.

Yet, like any aspect of marketing, harnessing intent signals comes with challenges and limitations. As we have mentioned numerous times, privacy concerns are a prominent issue that marketers must navigate carefully. With growing scrutiny around data collection and consumer privacy, it is essential to strike a balance between personalisation and respecting user boundaries. Moreover, intent signals can sometimes be misleading, leading to inaccuracies in targeting. The Privacy and Electronic Communication Regulations (PECR), for example, allow website visitors to turn off nonessential tracking cookies that may be used to collect data about their online behaviours. This means that not all visitors to a website are tracked, and the data generated is therefore not representative of the wider population.

To effectively leverage intent signals, marketers need to begin in the campaign-planning process, attempting to understand the buyer's journey and selecting keywords that align with user intent. Ad copywriting should be optimised, incorporating relevant keywords and compelling messaging that resonates with user desires. Landing pages should be crafted to deliver a seamless and personalised experience, ensuring that users are met with what they expect and are, therefore, more likely to convert into customers.

In conclusion, understanding and utilising intent signals in paid advertising is vital in today's digital landscape. The potential benefits are vast, from better audience targeting to improved ad relevance and reduced costs. However, navigating the challenges and limitations that come with intent signals is essential, ensuring that privacy is respected, and campaigns are continuously optimised.

Keyword Research for Paid Advertising

Keyword research plays a pivotal role in the success of paid advertising campaigns and, as with all other aspects of keyword research, involves identifying keywords that align with the target audience's intent. By understanding user intent, we can strategically select keywords that drive successful paid advertising campaigns.

This approach goes beyond surface-level keyword selection and delves into the mindset and desires of the users. By understanding the intent behind their search queries, we can create more relevant and targeted ads that resonate with them. This leads to higher click-through rates and, ultimately, more conversions.

It's not just the keywords directly linked to your product and service that are important in paid advertising. Your negative keywords (keywords and phrases that aren't relevant to your business and products/services) are also extremely valuable. In paid search advertising, you can enter negative keywords into the system as words you don't want your advert showing in response to. This simple action can help increase your advert's conversion rate and keep costs as low as possible by not being shown to users who type irrelevant queries into the search bar.

When carried out correctly, intent-focused keyword research is very successful and can generate positive results even if your budget is relatively low. One practical example of this is a Pay-Per-Click (PPC) campaign set up for a private residential landlord with six empty properties in Germany. By focusing on keywords with local and transactional intent and setting up the targeting correctly in the ads system, five of the six properties were let within eleven days of starting the ads (these conversions can be tracked directly to the PPC advertising) at a cost of just £4.07.

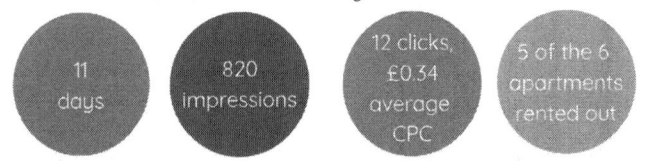

Figure 2: A case study of a PPC campaign using comprehensive keyword research and intent analysis.

Identifying high-converting keywords is crucial for the success of paid advertising campaigns. We can determine which keywords generate the most conversions by analysing conversion data and metrics. This allows us to allocate our budget and resources effectively to the keywords with the highest success potential. Additionally, through the continuous monitoring and refinement of keyword lists, we can optimise overall campaign performance.

Unlocking Search Intent

Ad Copy and Landing Page Optimisation for Intent

As well as finding the right keywords for Pay-Per-Click (PPC) advertising, the headline and tagline of our advertisements play a critical role in capturing the user's attention and enticing them to click through to our website.

Writing persuasive ad copy requires a deep understanding of our target audience and their pain points. We must address their needs, highlight the benefits of our product or service, and create a sense of urgency that prompts action. Employing proven copywriting techniques allows us to compellingly convey our message and propel users to take the desired action. We can improve overall campaign performance by genuinely connecting with our audience while fostering loyalty and trust.

A well-optimised landing page is crucial for converting ad clicks into meaningful actions. This requires aligning our landing page messaging with the user's intent, ensuring a seamless transition from the ad copy.

A persuasive ad and an optimised landing page are incomplete without a clear and compelling CTA. The CTA prompts the user to take the desired action, such as signing up for a newsletter or purchasing. By optimising our CTAs, we can increase conversion rates and maximise our return on investment.

Ad copy and landing page optimisation is an ongoing process that requires experimentation and continuous improvement. To truly harness the power of intent-based optimisation, we must be willing to test variations of our ad copy and landing pages. Through A/B testing, we can identify the most effective combinations and make data-driven decisions that drive superior results. We can refine and optimise our campaigns by analysing user behaviours, engagement metrics, and conversion rates to ensure long-term success. Just remember, when it comes to testing and changing content, try to change one variable at a time to make it easier to determine which changes prompted positive, and negative, results.

Ad Targeting and Intent-Based Segmentation

Ad targeting is a crucial aspect of modern marketing. It involves tailoring advertisements to specific audience segments to increase relevancy and improve overall ad performance. Through ad targeting, marketers can reach the right people with the right message at the right time, maximising the chances of conversion and driving business growth.

Demographic targeting is one of the most widely used methods of ad targeting. It involves segmenting audiences based on age, gender, location, and income. By understanding the demographic profile of their target audiences, marketers can create targeted ads that speak directly to their needs and desires.

The benefits of demographic targeting are vast. It allows marketers to reach specific audiences with precision and increase the relevancy of their ads. For example, a luxury skincare brand may want to target females between the ages of twenty-five and forty with a certain income level as they are more likely to be interested in high-end beauty products. By focusing ad spending on this specific demographic, the brand can maximise its return on investment and drive further sales.

Interest-based targeting takes ad targeting a step further by segmenting audiences based on their interests, hobbies, and online behaviours. By understanding what their target audience is interested in, marketers can tailor their ads to align with those interests and increase engagement.

Interest-based targeting offers several benefits. Firstly, it allows marketers to reach highly engaged audiences who are more likely to interact with their ads. For example, a sports brand may target individuals interested in running and fitness as they are more likely to be interested in their products. By catering to the specific interests of their target audience, the brand can increase the relevancy and effectiveness of their ads.

Intent-based segmentation takes ad targeting to the next level by understanding user intent and targeting specific audience segments. By analysing user behaviour, search queries, and other relevant data, marketers can identify the intent behind a user's actions and tailor their ads to align with that intent.

The benefits of intent-based segmentation are immense. Marketers can increase click-through rates, conversions, and overall campaign performance by targeting specific audience segments based on their intent. For example, a travel agency may want to target individuals searching for foreign holiday destinations as they are more likely to be interested in booking a trip. By aligning their ads with the intent of their target audience, the travel agency can increase their chances of conversion and revenue.

User intent plays a crucial role in ad performance. By understanding what users are looking for and tailoring ads to align with their intent, marketers can create more relevant and compelling ads that resonate with their target audience.

For example, a user searching for 'best running shoes for flat feet' is likely looking for information on running shoes that cater to that specific needs. By creating ads that address this intent and highlight relevant products, marketers can increase the chances of conversion. The key is to align the ad's messaging, visuals, and CTA with the user's intent, creating a seamless and seemingly personalised user experience.

Optimising ad campaigns with intent-based segmentation is a continuous process that requires constant monitoring and adjustment. Marketers can refine and optimise their ad campaigns by tracking key metrics and analysing user behaviour to improve overall performance. For example, if a marketer notices that specific audience segments are not responding well to their ads, they can adjust their targeting parameters to reach a more relevant audience. They can also experiment with different ad formats, messaging, and visuals to see what resonates best with the target audience. By continuously monitoring and adjusting their ad campaigns based on user intent, marketers can ensure that their ads are always relevant and effective.

Chapter 10

ETHICAL CONSIDERATIONS IN INTENT-BASED MARKETING

Privacy and Data Protection

According to Statista[4] (Statista, 2023), the average internet user in the United Kingdom spent 3.5 hours accessing the internet in June 2023. Spending so much time online isn't unusual, yet many internet users are unaware that their personal information is continuously collected and used by businesses for targeted marketing purposes. For this reason, privacy and data protection have become increasingly important over the last few years, particularly post-GDPR (the General Data Protection Regulations launched in the United Kingdom and Europe in May 2018).

Privacy, or the protection of personal information, plays a crucial role in shaping user intent. Users are gradually becoming more aware of the data being collected about them and, therefore, becoming more hesitant to engage

---

[4] UK: daily online time per person per device 2023 (2023). *Statista*. Available at: https://www.statista.com/statistics/477137/daily-time-spent-online-per-person-per-device-in-the-united-kingdom-uk/.

with intent-based marketing activities when they perceive their privacy could be compromised. Users may refrain from interacting with marketing campaigns or conducting transactions altogether when they feel that their personal information is at risk. This hesitation stems from a desire to protect their private lives and maintain control over their digital footprints. As a result, privacy can significantly impact user decision-making and behaviour in the online marketplace.

To build and maintain user trust, robust data protection measures are essential. The potential negative consequences of data breaches and misuse of user information are far-reaching with reputational damage, legal implications, and loss of customer loyalty, to name just a few examples. Organisations can enhance user confidence and improve overall marketing effectiveness by prioritising data protection. Users are more likely to engage with businesses they trust to handle their personal information responsibly, creating a mutually beneficial relationship between marketers and consumers.

Organisations must comply with privacy regulations and laws in the complex landscape of intent-based marketing. Data protection legislation, such as the GDPR and the California Consumer Privacy Act (CCPA), have established guidelines to safeguard user privacy rights. Organisations must ensure they are aware of and adhere to these regulations to protect their users and their interests. Implementing privacy policies and procedures is not merely a legal obligation but a demonstration of commitment to ethical marketing practices and user trust.

Realising the importance of safeguarding user information, organisations must employ practical strategies and best practices to maintain data security. Encryption, secure data storage, and access controls protect user data from unauthorised access or potential breaches. However, safeguarding user information extends beyond technical measures. Regular data audits and employee training are essential to maintaining robust data security practices. By keeping security protocols up-to-date and educating staff on privacy regulations, organisations can enhance their abilities to safeguard user information effectively.

Transparency is a fundamental aspect of intent-based marketing best practice. Organisations must adopt transparent data collection and usage practices to build user trust. Organisations can ensure users know how their information is being leveraged by clearly communicating how user data is collected, stored, and utilised. Furthermore, obtaining user consent and providing opt-out options aligns marketing practices with user privacy preferences. Respecting privacy choices strengthens user trust and fosters a positive relationship between marketers and users based on transparency and mutual understanding.

User education is pivotal in creating awareness about privacy and data protection in intent-based marketing. Organisations can support a more privacy-conscious user base by educating users about their rights and empowering them to make informed choices. Recommendations for user education include providing clear and concise privacy policies, offering user-friendly explanations of data collection practices, and facilitating access to additional privacy and data protection resources. This increased awareness empowers users to take control of their personal information and make conscious decisions about which marketing practices they engage with.

In the pursuit of enforcing high privacy standards, collaboration between marketers, industry associations, and regulatory bodies is paramount. The entire digital marketing ecosystem benefits by sharing best practices and collaborating on privacy initiatives. Marketers can learn from each other's experiences and collectively work towards preserving user privacy. Self-regulation and voluntary standards also play a crucial role in maintaining high privacy standards.

Privacy and data protection are not optional components of intent-based marketing. They are vital aspects that shape user trust, inform user intent, and ultimately drive purchasing decisions. Organisations must prioritise user privacy and adapt their policies and practices to align with changing regulations and user expectations. Safeguarding user information, building transparency, educating users, and collaborating with industry stakeholders are ongoing commitments that will solidify user trust and enable ethical and effective intent-based marketing practices. As digital marketers, business owners, and professionals, we are responsible for promoting privacy and data protection as cornerstones of our industry, offering users a safe and trustworthy online experience.

User Consent and Opt-Out Options

Before we can dive into the practicalities of user consent and opt-out options, it is essential to understand the legal requirements and regulations surrounding intent-based marketing. Laws such as the GDPR and the CCPA have been enacted to enforce the need for transparent consent practices. These regulations provide strict guidelines regarding what constitutes valid consent, clearly informing users of data collection and usage, and the importance of allowing users to control their personal data. By adhering to these legal requirements, marketers can ensure that their marketing practices are lawful, ethical, and in line with the best interests of their users.

To obtain valid and informed consent from users, it is crucial to design consent forms that are clear, easy to understand, and transparent. Plain language should be used, avoiding complex jargon that may confuse or mislead users. Consent forms should provide options for different types of consent, allowing users to choose the level of personalisation and data sharing they are comfortable with. Furthermore, it is essential to ensure that users are fully informed about the data they provide and the purposes for which it will be used. This transparency builds trust and empowers users to make informed decisions about their data.

Intent-based marketing must prioritise obtaining informed consent from users. This goes beyond merely acquiring a user's consent to collect and use their data; it involves educating users about the purposes and consequences of their consent. Marketers should use explicit consent mechanisms, ensuring users actively indicate their agreement rather than relying on pre-ticked boxes or implied consent. By clearly explaining the benefits of data sharing and its potential risks, marketers can enable users to make informed choices about their data and align their preferences with the marketing messages they receive.

While obtaining consent is crucial, providing users with opt-out options and giving them control over their personal data and marketing preferences is equally important. Opt-out mechanisms should be clear, easily accessible, and actioned promptly by marketers. Users should be able to update their preferences and opt out of certain marketing communications or data sharing anytime. By respecting users' choices and giving them control, marketers can foster a sense of empowerment, build trust, and maintain a positive relationship with their audiences.

Avoiding Manipulation and Deception

Manipulative and deceptive marketing tactics can have a profoundly negative impact on trust, customer relationships, and a brand's overall reputation. When marketers resort to such tactics, they harm the consumer and jeopardise their long-term success. As professionals in the field, we have an ethical responsibility to ensure that our marketing practices are transparent, honest, and respectful of customer autonomy.

The harms of manipulative marketing extend far beyond the immediate transaction. By employing tactics meant to deceive or manipulate consumers into making uninformed purchasing decisions, marketers risk buyer's remorse and foster a sense of mistrust and disillusionment in the marketing industry as a whole. This loss of trust affects not only the brand being marketed but also the industry.

On the other hand, prioritising ethical considerations in marketing strategies brings numerous benefits. By building trust and fostering long-term customer relationships, marketers can create brand loyalty and turn customers into advocates who spread positive word-of-mouth information about the brand. Ethical marketing tactics create a positive customer experience, enhancing a brand's reputation and contributing to the overall positive perception of the marketing industry.

To avoid falling into the trap of manipulative and deceptive tactics, it's good to learn from the mistakes of others. These examples serve as cautionary tales from false advertising and misleading claims to hidden fees and fine print. They highlight the importance of avoiding these tactics and instead focus on building customer trust through ethical marketing practices.

Bias in Search-Intent Analysis

Bias in search-intent analysis is a complex and multifaceted issue that, though we have touched on it briefly already, deserves careful examination and explanation. As a researcher, I am acutely aware of the significance of understanding biases in search results and user experiences. Algorithmic bias and data bias are potential sources of bias that must be addressed in search-intent analysis.

Algorithmic bias refers to biases embedded within the algorithms used by search engines to generate search results. These biases can arise from the algorithms' design or the data used to train them. For example, if a search engine's algorithm is designed to prioritise certain types of content or sources, it may inadvertently exclude or downplay other perspectives, leading to a biased representation of information. This can have a profound impact on search-intent analysis as users rely on search results to inform their decision-making processes and shape their understanding of the world.

Addressing algorithmic bias in search-intent analysis is

crucial for ensuring fair and unbiased search results. Search engine providers must constantly evaluate and refine their algorithms to mitigate bias and promote a more inclusive and diverse representation of information. This requires ongoing research and collaboration between technologists, content creators, and users to develop algorithms prioritising accuracy, fairness, and impartiality.

Data bias is another source of bias in the search-intent analysis. Data bias refers to biases that arise from the data used to train algorithms or generate search results. If the data used is not representative of users' diverse perspectives and experiences, it can lead to a skewed and incomplete understanding of user intent. This can result in search results favouring specific demographics or reinforcing existing societal biases and inequalities.

Examples of data bias in search results are widespread. Research has shown that search results for certain health conditions, for example, tend to prioritise information that is more readily available and represented in the data rather than consider a comprehensive range of perspectives and experiences. This can have severe consequences for individuals seeking accurate and reliable health information as they may be presented with a limited and potentially biased view of their condition.

Addressing data bias in search-intent analysis requires diverse and inclusive data sets. Search engine providers must actively seek and incorporate a wide range of perspectives and experiences to ensure that search results accurately reflect users' diverse needs and interests. Additionally, leveraging AI and machine-learning technologies can help improve search-intent analysis by identifying and mitigating biases in the data. Identifying and addressing biases in search-intent analysis presents numerous challenges. Biases can lead to unequal access to information and reinforce societal biases, perpetuating inequalities and limiting individuals' abilities to make informed decisions.

Diverse data sets and inclusive algorithms are essential to mitigate biases in search-intent analysis. By incorporating various perspectives and experiences, search engine providers can reduce bias and deliver more representative search results. AI and machine-learning technologies can also play a crucial role in improving search-intent analysis by identifying and addressing biases in real time.

The impact of bias on user trust and satisfaction with search results cannot be overstated. Biased search-intent analysis can lead to distorted perceptions of reality and affect user decision-making and information-seeking behaviours. Ultimately, biased search-intent analysis can have long-term effects on society, perpetuating inequality and reinforcing existing biases. Therefore, it is imperative to recognise the importance of unbiased search-intent analysis in fostering a more equitable and inclusive digital world.

It's important to note that the responsibility of addressing biases in search-intent analysis falls on search engine providers and regulators. Search engine providers must take it upon themselves to ensure fair and unbiased search results. Still, regulators also have a role to play in establishing frameworks and guidelines to mitigate biases. Collaborative efforts between search engine providers and regulators are essential in addressing biases and ensuring that search-intent analysis is conducted ethically and responsibly.

As we look to the future, there are challenges and opportunities in addressing biases in search-intent analysis. Emerging technologies such as NLP and AI systems hold great promise in reducing biases and improving search-intent analysis. However, careful consideration must be given to the potential impact of these technologies, and ongoing research and collaboration are crucial to ensure that search-intent analysis remains unbiased and beneficial in the age of AI. We can build a digital landscape that truly serves all individuals and fosters equality, understanding, and progress by continuously striving for unbiased search-intent analysis.

Responsible Use of AI in Search-Intent Analysis

Accountability is a fundamental aspect that must permeate every stage of AI-driven search-intent analysis. From the initial development of the algorithms to the deployment and use of AI technologies, developers, companies, and stakeholders are responsible for ensuring ethical practices. Users place their trust in search engines to provide them with accurate and unbiased results, and as such, the accountability lies with those creating and managing these AI systems. Negligence or disregard for ethical considerations can result in detrimental consequences, undermining user trust and perpetuating biases.

Fairness is another crucial concern in AI-driven search-intent analysis. Fairness is multifaceted and extends beyond merely providing equal opportunities for all users. Biased algorithms and search results can have far-reaching ramifications, perpetuating inequalities and reinforcing existing prejudices. Research has repeatedly proven that search results are not immune to biases, often favouring specific demographics or presenting users with limited and potentially skewed perspectives. To ensure fairness, search engine providers must embrace diversity and inclusivity in their data sets, allowing for a more comprehensive understanding of user intent and information needs.

The potential harmful consequences of using AI technologies without considering ethical factors should not be underestimated. As search-intent analysis increasingly relies on AI systems, concerns regarding user privacy, data security, and overall user experience emerge. AI systems possess an unparalleled ability to collect and analyse vast amounts of data, often without users' explicit knowledge. This raises profound questions regarding the ethical handling and utilisation of personal data. Responsible practices necessitate a proactive approach, placing privacy and data security at the forefront of activities. Only through vigilant attention to these concerns can we ensure that AI-driven search-intent analysis enhances user experiences without compromising their privacy rights.

Practical guidelines must be established to ensure the responsible use of AI in search-intent analysis. These guidelines should emphasise transparency and accountability in AI algorithms and models. Search engine providers must be transparent about their data collection and processing methods and the principles guiding their AI systems. Additionally, developing frameworks or guidelines specific to the ethical deployment of AI in search-intent analysis can provide valuable guidance to organisations and researchers in this field. By adhering to such guidelines, stakeholders can uphold their responsibility to use AI technologies in an ethical and accountable manner.

Free Will and AI

Whilst considering the ethics of intent-based marketing, it is worth mentioning the debate concerning the impact of AI on human thought and decision-making from a philosophical perspective. In a world increasingly influenced by AI, personalisation, and digital information overload, we find ourselves at the crossroads between philosophy and technology. When we are presenting information that a user wants or needs, it requires us to take away stages of the natural, human decision-making process. So are convenience and user experience hurting our free will?

In philosophy, the notion of free will encompasses debates on determinism, moral responsibility, and the perceived autonomy of human actions. At the other end of the spectrum, AI and algorithms exist within a framework of rules, preprogrammed decisions, and artificial models of human behaviour.

The inquiry into free will traces its roots back to ancient philosophical discourse. Early thinkers such as Aristotle, Plato, and Socrates grappled with the fundamental question of human agency and the capacity for autonomous decision-making. The concept of free will has transcended time and culture, shaping moral and ethical frameworks across civilisations.

The debate on free will has experienced pivotal milestones throughout history, each contributing to its evolving narrative. The rise of Christianity in the Middle Ages in Europe saw intense discussions on predestination and free will as theologians grappled with the interplay between divine sovereignty and human agency. The Enlightenment era ushered in a resurgence of interest in free will as thinkers like Immanuel Kant sought to reconcile rational autonomy with the deterministic forces of nature.

The advent of modern neuroscience in the twentieth century brought a major shift in the understanding of human cognition and behaviour. Pioneering work in neuroscience introduced empirical investigations into the neural processes underlying decision-making, challenging traditional notions of free will. Advancements in neuroimaging have raised questions about the extent to which brain activity predetermines human choices, precipitating debates on the compatibility of free will with neuroscientific findings.

Despite the debate on the accuracy and legitimacy of the concept of free will, it remains a widely held understanding that our independent thought processes are what makes us inherently human.

> I am no bird, and no net ensnares me: I am a free human being with an independent will.
>
> —Charlotte Brontë in *Jane Eyre*

When it comes to AI content generation tools and human-authored content in the search engine results pages, are they so different? Both aim to convey information with a specific purpose, whether to inform, persuade, or entertain. When it comes to creating inspiring and engaging content tailored to a user's intent, both types of content share common ground as both human- and AI-generated content generally strive to meet the demands of search engine algorithms and user expectations.

However, the growth of algorithmically generated content in SERPs has caused concern about the potential erosion of human agency and the commodification of information. Some argue that human-authored content bears the imprint of individual thought, creativity, and subjective experience, embodying the essence of free will as expressed through creation. In stark contrast, they perceive

AI-generated content as an output of predetermined algorithms devoid of subjective consciousness or the capacity for autonomous volition. The reality is that both can provide insightful, relevant content or biased, inaccurate information depending on the source data used to inspire the content. It's just that, as users, we are unaware of whether humans or machines are influencing us and are, therefore, unable to consider that variable as we review and digest the content we are presented with and make purchase decisions based on that information.

The landscape of digital marketing and SEO is constantly evolving, driven by advancements in artificial intelligence and machine-learning algorithms. These technologies have allowed us to generate vast volumes of content with unprecedented speed and efficiency. However, some still fear that the erosion of human agency in content creation could lead to a homogenisation of digital expression, diluting the richness and diversity of human perspectives. In addition, the uncritical dissemination of AI-generated content in SERPs may perpetuate biases and reinforce existing power structures, undermining the principles of fairness and equity. As a result, we must undertake marketing activities, particularly those involving data collection, AI, or emotional manipulation, thoughtfully and carefully if we want to be ethical marketers.

Chapter 11

THE PRACTICAL APPLICATION OF INTENT-BASED KEYWORD RESEARCH

As we come to the end of this book, it's worth reviewing some of the critical points we have discussed on our journey. As business owners, digital marketers, and business professionals, we know that there isn't a single linear journey that takes customers from finding out about a product or service to purchasing it. We all have different motivations, goals, challenges, and intentions. So why do so many businesses try to appeal to all customers in the same way? By optimising content for informational, transactional, navigational, commercial investigation, or local intent, we can effectively engage our specific audiences and guide them towards their desired actions. This starts with finding the keyword phrases they are searching for online through intensive and comprehensive keyword research and then reviewing that list to determine the associated search intent for each phrase.

Another common thread throughout this book has been the issue of AI algorithmic bias and researcher bias (our own inherent and subjective interpretation of an idea or situation). Keyword research and user intent analysis are never going to be 100 per cent accurate, whether we use an AI tool or our human experiences to categorise keywords based on intent. However, some analysis is always better than none, particularly if you are aware of the potential limitations of research and take steps to address them. In addition, with careful monitoring of metrics such as reach, click-through rate, engagement rate, conversion rate, and so on, we can make a more informed decision about whether or not our categorisations (based on intent) and our associated optimisation work are accurate. If it is, that's great! If it's not, we know better for next time and can work to refine our categorisation and optimisation. As with all digital marketing activities, keyword research and search intent analyses need to be involved in a cycle of continuous refinement and improvement.

Finally, when it comes to the all-important activity of keyword research, if you are going to engage in it, make sure you allocate time—and brain power—to it. There are free keyword research tools out there, but many lack details like monthly search volume and associated CPC, which means you are missing out on valuable insights. As mentioned, I recommend the keyword research tool https://keywordstrategytool.com/ for comprehensive keyword research, a resource developed as an in-house tool for our digital marketing agency five years ago. The tool offers users a free seven-day trial to help you start compiling your detailed keyword list and begin the journey towards determining user intent online and tailoring your website, online ads, and content to the needs and motivations of potential customers.

To finish, I'm pleased to showcase another brief case study from our digital marketing agency, Digital Groundwork, that shows the impact that search-intent-focused, comprehensive keyword research can have on a business's conversion rates.

This case study is of an online retailer in the United Kingdom in the health/wellbeing sector. Support for this business began in May 2023. It included comprehensive keyword research with a strong focus on consumer search intent followed by SEO of their products with relevant purchase intent keywords, the addition of blogs and social content with a focus on informational intent keywords, and a refreshed paid search advertising campaign driven by all the research into consumer intent. Here are some of the results:

- Average CPC is down 50 per cent over the six-month period and has an increased reach of 200 per cent based on an equivalent budget for that same period.
- Averaging 5 to 8 per cent click-through rate across all Google Ad campaigns.
- A 75 per cent increase in orders compared to the previous six-month period.

At the end of six months of support from our team, the business had increased total gross sales by £125,608, increased their average monthly sales by 39 per cent, and generated a 29x return on marketing investment, with the only change made in their marketing activities attributed to the keyword research, SEO, PPC advertising, and content marketing recommendations.

As you can see, keyword research is the key to unlocking search intent and understanding consumer motivations online. In this age of digital information overload, the simple things— listening to your customers' needs, goals, and challenges—will set you apart in the search results for all the right reasons. I hope you can adopt some of the ideas and techniques mentioned in this book in your digital marketing activities, helping to build positive relationships with website visitors, potential customers, and existing customers based on their unique intentions. Good luck!

Chapter 12
DIGITAL MARKETING GLOSSARY

Digital marketing is known for its acronyms and jargon, so although I haven't used all of these within this book, I have included a short glossary to help you navigate the linguistic challenges of this subject.

AR (Augmented Reality) is a technology that superimposes a computer-generated image on the user's view of the real world.

B2B (Business-to-Business) is a communication/relationship between two different businesses.

B2C (Business-to-Customer) is a communication/relationship between a customer and a business.

BR (Bounce Rate) is the percentage of the people who land on your webpage and return within three seconds.

CAPTCHA (Completely Automated Public Turing Test to Tell Computers and Humans Apart) is a method to check whether the user is a person or a robot.

CMS (Content Management System) is a Web application specifically designed to make the process of creating, editing, and managing a website easy for nontechnical users.

CPA (Cost Per Action) is a model in which an advertiser pays only for the action someone takes like a click, impression, or sale.

CPC (Cost Per Click) is the amount of money spent to get an ad clicked when running PPC campaigns.

CPL (Cost Per Lead) is the amount it costs for your organisation to acquire a lead.

CR (Conversion Rate) refers to the people who completed the desired action on a webpage, such as making a purchase or filling in a form.

CRO (Conversion Rate Optimisation) is the process of optimising your website (that is, by enhancing the design of your website) to increase conversion rates.

CRM (Customer Relationship Management) is the relationship of your business with the customers. CRM systems hold data about your customers and can be linked with an email marketing platform.

CTA (Call to Action) refers to the action button to, for example, sign up, subscribe, purchase, like, or follow.

CTR (Click-through Rate) is a percentage calculated by comparing the number of clicks on a CTA with the total number of people who could have clicked on it; that is, the number of people who saw the advert or CTA.

CX (Customer Experience) is the customer's experience with the organisation.

KPI (Key Performance Indicator) is one (or many) metrics you need to monitor to determine the success of your marketing activities.

LTV (Lifetime Value) is the average value of a customer for their entire life cycle with you.

PPC (Pay Per Click) refers to advertising via Google/Bing ads, and so on, where potential customers click on an advert, and you are charged for that action.

ROI (Return on Investment) / ROMI (Return on Marketing Investment) is a calculation that determines how much money you have made as a direct result of a marketing activity when compared to the cost of implementing that marketing activity.

SEO (Search Engine Optimisation) refers to the optimisation of your website to be ranked more highly in the SERPs.

SERPs (Search Engine Result Pages) are the pages that are shown by the search engine when a user searches for some keywords.

SMM (Social Media Marketing) is the use of social media platforms to promote a product or service.

UI (User Interface) is the way a website or app interacts with a user. A good user interface provides user-friendly experiences by allowing users to interact easily and effectively with the website/app.

URL (Uniform Resource Locator) is the web address of a website, for example, www.mywebsite.co.uk.

UX (User Experience) is the overall experience a customer has with your business, website, and so on.

VR (Virtual Reality) is a computer-generated simulation or a 3D image or environment with which a user can interact.

About the Author

Gemma Pybus is an experienced digital marketer with a deep interest in consumer psychology. As a senior lecturer at the University of West London, digital marketing trainer, and director of Digital Groundwork Ltd., Gemma and the Digital Groundwork team specialise in the essential foundations of digital marketing—keyword research, PPC advertising, SEO, and content marketing. Gemma also has extensive experience as a technical copywriter and sales and marketing automation specialist.

Over the last decade, Gemma has collaborated with an eclectic range of businesses, from worm farms to international airlines (and what feels like everything in between, including legal contracts and owls), gaining insights into the diverse digital landscapes that shape online success. She firmly believes that keyword research, often underestimated, is a pivotal factor in achieving significant digital marketing outcomes, which is why she felt compelled to put pen to paper and write this book.

Living in Aylesbury with her husband, James Pybus, a fellow digital marketing specialist and PPC wizard, Gemma and James juggle their professional pursuits with the joys of parenthood, raising three fantastic children along with a cat named Jeff, a rabbit named Neil, a hamster named Colin, and a dynamic aquatic team of goldfish and sea-monkeys.

Gemma and James's dedication to advancing

digital marketing practices led them to create their own comprehensive keyword research tool, https://keywordstrategytool.com/. This innovative tool earned them recognition, winning the Best Marketing Management Tool at the B2B Expo at London's ExCeL Centre in 2019. This isn't the only award on their bookshelf (alongside children's toys). In 2022, Gemma was named runner-up at the Everywoman in Technology Awards in their STEM Academic of the Year category. And in 2023, Gemma was named by Business Elite Awards as one of their 40 Under 40 European Business Leaders at a very fancy event in Türkiye.

Printed and bound by CPI Group (UK) Ltd, Croydon, CR0 4YY